This Tilted World Is Where I Live

This Tilted World Is Where I Live

New and Selected Poems, 1962–2020

Henry Taylor

Louisiana State University Press
Baton Rouge

Published by Louisiana State University Press
www.lsupress.org

Manufactured in the United States of America
First printing

Designer: Barbara Neely Bourgoyne
Typeface: Whitman
Printer and binder: Sheridan Books

Library of Congress Cataloging-in-Publication Data

Names: Taylor, Henry, 1942– author.
Title: This tilted world is where I live : new and selected poems, 1962–2020 / Henry Taylor.
Description: Baton Rouge : Louisiana State University Press, 2020.
Identifiers: LCCN 2020001274 (print) | LCCN 2020001275 (ebook) | ISBN 978-0-8071-7177-6 (cloth) | ISBN 978-0-8071-7178-3 (paperback) | ISBN 978-0-8071-7415-9 (pdf) | ISBN 978-0-8071-7416-6 (epub)
Classification: LCC PS3570.A93 T55 2020 (print) | LCC PS3570.A93 (ebook) | DDC 811/.54—dc23
LC record available at https://lccn.loc.gov/2020001274
LC ebook record available at https://lccn.loc.gov/2020001275

For Mooshe

I love to watch you track your knowing hand
among the skeins arranged in a yarn store,
gauging the blend's effect, plucking a strand
to try the feature you've been hunting for.
I love how you speak to strangers on the phone,
listening for the way to where they are,
so you can make that space a safety zone
from which no understanding seems too far.
You praise the beauty of a checkout girl
while I stand wondering which way to look
as the checker blushes and flicks back a curl.
This miracle, however long it took
to become you, is daily. You set your course
by steadfast signals from the universe.

CONTENTS

II. Crooked Run (1996–2006)

III. Understanding Fiction (1986–1996)

IV. The Flying Change (1974–1985)

VI. The Horse Show at Midnight (1963–1966)

AUTHOR'S NOTE

The years indicating periods covered by the sections are those of first publication of the earliest and latest poems in each.

Only a very small number of relatives and friends have been with me longer than I have been with LSU Press. For more than fifty years, people there have been earning my deep gratitude and admiration. This time around, for sensitive care in the production of the book, I want to thank Kate Barton, Erica Bossier, Barbara Neely Bourgoyne, LB Kovac, James Long, Neal Novak, and James Wilson.

I

Yesterdays: New Poems
(1998–2020)

The Living Room at Springdale

Mentally enter a long-remembered room
and note which of its features have withdrawn
in favor of a handful of details
that sharpen—do they change?—as decades pass.

Above the mantel the carved picture frame
encloses formless drifts of shifting hues;
the carpet blinks from figured Oriental
to solid gray, and back again. The wall

around the fireplace: Was it papered? Painted?
You came in from the hallway and looked left.
Whatever may have stood in the rightward end
is simply gone; its shadowy non-space

will not give up the objects it contained.
Yet here is the leather chair whose dented cushion
you can still feel as you settled in beside
the phonograph that spun a seventy-eight—

the voice of a melodramatic actor
reciting snips of *Julius Caesar* and *Hamlet*,
the first time in your life, you now believe,
that you heard the question whether or not to be.

Hay by the Calendar

A man we knew made hay by the calendar.
From almanacs and long experience
he marked the dates to cut, rake, and bale up.

Sometimes we saw him mowing through the rain,
his plaid shirt and the cushioned tractor seat
more deeply soaked with every steady round.

We weather-sniffers might have been amused
when he baled spoiled windrows just to clear the field,
but not when rainstorms doused our sun-dried swaths.

He let us be, and did his work his way
until he died, and left us here to wonder
who, through all those seasons, made more good hay.

I Thought She Said

"I have to finish one more parrot bath."
My mind stalled out on water, dusty wings,
green feathers floating in a soapy tub.
That time, I'm glad to say, I didn't speak
before I knew that she meant "paragraph."
That "paragraph," I mean, is what she'd said.

My mind slipped into gear and drifted by
a bird I actually met one afternoon
while I was waiting for a wheel alignment.
Beyond the crackling Naugahyde I sat on,
out in the service bay, I heard the ring,
sharp as the first bite of a winter apple,

of a tire iron on concrete. Did Gary Snyder,
maybe, say poetry should sound like that?
Six more times in thirty minutes. Finally
I made a smart remark about slippery tools,
and the woman working behind the counter said,
"It's the bird." Was that really what she'd said?

She glanced over her shoulder as if to say
I could get up and go see for myself.
I looked in a back room, and there he was,
pacing his dowel perch: a myna bird.
"He learned to make that noise last month," she said,
"and we can't hardly tell the difference."

Silo

From dinner with my sisters at the farm
I walked out through the back yard just at dusk,
down toward the dairy, to what we had called
"the new silo" for more than forty years,
it being the only concrete silo on the place.
They laid the jointed blocks to forty-five feet,
a thin steel ladder bolted to the side,
a crow's nest at the top. You entered it

by lifting the net-steel platform like a trap door,
climbing through, settling it back into its frame,
then standing on it. When I was about twelve,
that was one of the places I needed to be.
From up there I could watch how the barnyard
fitted between the barn's end and the shop.
Now against the sky the big silo loomed,
and it came to me to try the climb, to see

if I still could. I had taken care enough
as a boy, had never slipped, but now I was
cautious almost to a fault, speaking aloud
each step in the procedure, when I saw
that years had opened a gap in the domed roof,
and I could see across to the other side
where, on the concrete ledge, a slim barn owl
stared without blinking from its heart-shaped head.

It made a quick short lean in my direction,
combining a greeting and a closer look,
dropped from the ledge into the dark, then rose
toward me, wings snapped shut for the exit hole,
pulled a swift breeze across the top of my head
as mind and reflex argued with each other
whether to hold on or let go, and soared
into a darkling absence that abides.

A Persuasive Chill

One of my grandfather's stories

There was this lad, a Nichols, who was sweet
on a young woman in the neighborhood.
Her parents dead, she lived with a guardian,
Aunt Hattie, a stiff old Quaker lady
who held firmly to plain speech at all times.
Nichols was afraid of her, so he called
on his good friend Samuel Whitaker,
who stayed in Aunt Hattie's good graces
and could maybe put in a word for him.
So one day soon Samuel went by the house
and was admitted by a servant girl
who had him follow her into the parlor
and offered him a seat there. He said later
that as he sat he had one of those moments
where the sunlight on the chair-rail eased him
into a vision of the Meeting House,
and he stared at the spare but elegant wall
almost as if he were drifting into
the receptive state of silent worship.
In due time the old woman swept in, and he
jumped up: "Aunt Hattie, do I have thy chair?"
"Keep thy seat, Samuel. All the chairs are mine."

The Ages

Someone asks every now and then whether
technical words can doom a poem
to early extinction. It's an odd question,
given the myriad other ways a poet
can produce stupefying ephemera.

Meanwhile, a glitch in my installation
of Word 2010 for Windows has led me
to the support phones, and I am talking
to a gentleman in Delhi (I myself
am in Santa Fe, glancing at reports
of Muhammad Ali's death) and he, the excellent
Amal Kumar, asks if he may take control
of my computer. I've been here before,
and say yes. The software comes aboard,
I click the consent box, and the cursor
skids away on what looks like its own,
but Amal knows his stuff, and soon
has things straightened out. Word is
reinstalled afresh, and I'm in business.

I knew of a student once, from maybe Spain
or eastern Europe, her accent being nearly
imperceptible except at certain moments
in the workshop, when a poem would contain
a word such as "Revlon" or "motherboard,"
and her accent asserted itself
as she made her pronouncement: "It is
a very nice poem, but it is not for the ages."

Rarely, when I consider the ages,
I remember standing in a panelled room
in an Italianate villa on Afton Mountain,
between Charlottesville and Waynesboro.

For fifty years it was the home of Walter
and Lao Russell and their University
of Science and Philosophy. Walter
painted early in his career, and in 1900
produced "The Might of Ages," which
in 1964 hung on the aforesaid panelling
before my eyes. The large painting depicts
a kind of river of humanity descending
what might be a stair that ends on a balcony
overlooking a real river with boats in it,
a bridge across it, and a great city
on the other shore. The people in the foreground
are recognizable, or seem as if they might be.
I remember spotting Shakespeare, Socrates
(or was that Homer?), Washington, Lincoln. . . .
Many pictures are better than that one,
but somewhat fewer are more memorable.
It hangs now in a gallery in Blacksburg,
among other remnants of the University
of Science and Philosophy, and is at this writing
116 years old, which isn't all that much
as masterpieces go, but it's a start.

Bird-Call at Evening

Wherever we are, we find our wonderlands.
  In one small town, as we held hands
and strolled from dinner to our B & B,
  somewhere past roof and darkening tree
  a bird-call rose: *Bo peep, how sweet!*
I whistled back, and so we parleyed down the street.
  "What bird is that?" you asked, and I,
"What bird? That's just another sixtyish old guy."

You Don't Know All the Places You Take Me To

You look up from your book. "Who was Delmore Schwartz?"
So I look up from mine, say something about
the heavy bear, the bed in Plato's cave,
the sad end, and, pausing, recall a glimpse
of Delmore Schwartz walking up the left aisle
of the old Coolidge Auditorium
in October of 1962,
a cigarette (not in those days forbidden)
between his fingers and between his lips,
the ember burning with such ferocity
that sparks and ash-flecks danced away from it
as if it were itself a thing alive,
almost beyond the fierce control of the poet
who meanwhile tilted his face away from smoke
and squinted ahead, proceeding to the exit.

Ultrasound

The lights are dim in the examining room
so the nurse running the test can see her screen,
and maybe so the patient can more easily relax
as the ultrasound knob massages his abdomen.
Some sort of music is being piped in—
could it be a shakuhachi and a piano?
Inoffensive, potentially soothing, and yet
because the beeps and occasional growls
of the ultrasound machine are laid over it
in a pattern that seems random but may
only be chaotic, John Cage comes to mind,
and his love of almost any sound.

Years ago, in the mid- or late fifties, on what
television program it is hard to say,
he and a friend puttered cheerfully around
in what looked like a basement rec room—
bare pipes along the ceiling and down one wall,
a ping-pong table with a few tools on it,
a piano—around which they wandered,
scraping the table's legs on the concrete floor,
whacking the pipes with one tool or another,
plucking the piano strings, inventing
music, Cage radiating a nearly fixed smile
in an attitude tinged with mild mania.

Not much later, on a popular show
called "I've Got a Secret," the host asked him
to understand his audience. "Some of them
are going to laugh," he said, and Cage replied,
"I consider laughter preferable to tears."

Three decades on, to 1991, when
CageFest, an evening chamber concert, played

in Washington. Four pieces, intermission,
then one, the premiere of *Two*^{4}, for violin
and piano, a weirdly inviting slow set
of sounds that ask much of the violinist,
who must hold sharps and flats with human
steadiness for lengths of time it is hard
not to exaggerate in memory, the stretched tones
wavering as if they could disappear behind
themselves, as meanwhile isolated notes
from the piano drop into the procession
like leaves a breeze might lift across a stream.

Cage took questions afterwards, and at last
somebody got around to the new piece,
wondering which of Cage's famous chance
or random methods, what idea, determined
the length of that last piece. "I determined it.
I used the . . . idea . . . of thirty minutes."

Now lights come on, the nurse coils up the cords
of the machine, the patient pulls himself
to a sitting position and steps to the floor,
thinking less of his own heart than of John Cage's,
its rugged, bright defiance of gravity.

Two Winter Landscapes

A brown-backed flicker risks
a second-base slide
into the juniper outside
the window beyond our desk,

the white rump and brown wing feathers
mimicking until he matches
the bare trees and snow patches
on the far hill together.

Rockwell Kent on Monhegan Island

Cold light on rock would call his hands to work
when pot-buoys leapt and wavered in first light
and men who rose in dark, slickered for work,
drew close to shore, abstracted in their work
of hauling pots, indifferent to the cold.
He watched them, insulated from such work.
He traced the essential motion of their work
against a solid backdrop wall of rock,
seeking the line between motion and rock,
and strained to feel what drove men to the work
of pulling food from waves. He watched their hands,
ashamed of his thin wrists, his artist's hands.

He took to the boats himself, laying his hands
to frigid, salty lines. Lobstermen's work
suited his spirit more than it did his hands,
but he thought, those evenings when he thawed his hands
before his coalstove door's disturbing light,
that he had been created with two hands
for the world's use, to live by his own hands,
build his own house, and seal it from the cold.
He trained his eyes on light as it turned cold,
to a stillness he could capture in his hands
when he got the colors right and made the rock
seem to partake of sky, and sky of rock.

In errant moments he imagined rock
achieving permanence. Deep in his hands
there was the memory of drilling rock
the year he blasted wells and graves from rock
for an islander who saw his gift for work.
Now there were days when he painted a rock
lifting itself to air, more air than rock,
flowing along with the black waves whose light

swells rocked a dory's hull in scattered light.
He brushed a cap of snow across the rock
to see how it divided cold from cold,
the sky above and rock below. In cold

sunlight his nerves surged to embrace the cold,
as if to put down roots into the rock
like spruces crisping in the jeweled cold.
He came to see more sharply through the cold,
and the stiff air was seasoning for his hands.
He never renounced the notion that this cold
world demands real work, like heaving from the cold
the sustenance that fed his chosen work.
Meanwhile his hands turned firmly to new work,
having as much to gather from the cold
as men who pulled on oilskins by lamplight
and stooped above the waves in metallic light.

Fresh ecstasies of apprehended light
skidded down steep slate roofs and met the cold.
Umber and snow became a wash of light,
one of the ways paint had of making light
the weight of sun and water on the rock
looming, even in the faintest starlight,
as black as if it had devoured the light
that he could still feel pulsing in his hands.
Almost involuntarily, his hands
preserved the flash when a rising bow caught light,
then skipped it over shoulders stooped to work
in the flow of time, which it was his work

to interrupt, set down, and put to work.
That island brought his eyes in touch with light
and the textures air derived from sea and cold.
Labor and vision stood firm on one rock
as cold work drew the rock's light from his hands.

Walk On, Boys

At an RV park once, a woman was watching
as I walked our two English Goldendoodles
in a twelve-foot circle at the ends of their leashes,
sometimes letting them trot or run, and she said,
"They're like ponies on a longe line." It saves my steps
and tones them up and down at the same time.

I say to them, when I want them to get to it,
"Walk on, boys," and they pay attention.
When I hear myself say that, it takes me back
to the front yard of my sister's house in Virginia,
where, years ago, I found a coach-and-four pulled up
by the driveway, my father and sister talking
to the driver, who turned out to be Bill Dreyer,
our new neighbor over on the Lincoln road.

At least I now remember a four-in-hand;
it could be that a two-horse team that day
radiated enough dash and brilliance
to double themselves in my memory. Either way,
there was more than a little nobility in that team.
The visit concluded, he spoke those words,
and the horses moved off, eased into a trot,
and vanished while we could still hear their hooves.
Thereafter we saw him often on those roads.

He brought a touch of learned elegance
to the horse country that had been my home.
No one needs such driving now except for art,
and an artist is exactly what he was.
A few years later he died in a foxhunting accident,
and the coach's wheels stopped rolling through
our countryside. But almost every day, sometimes

more than once, I speak to the dogs as they circle
on their leashes, and thanks rise in me for Bill Dreyer,
for his responsive team and splendid coach,
for my having been there to see what he could do.

Drop Us From Our Day

After so many years I'm almost accustomed
to passing him as he steps toward the road's edge
from within the border of a diamond-shaped yellow sign:
all black, no hands or feet or neck, a round
and eyeless head. He often makes me think
of that great Addams cartoon, the driver's stricken face
in the left foreground, staring past the sign
at the human-sized family of round-headed
flat black neckless people walking rigidly
down off the curb and into the street.
For decades he has perfected his silent warnings.

During the final days of 2001, I saw him
in hard hotel light between two elevator doors,
frozen in the familiar stride, but tilted
perilously forward, his trailing leg shortened
the better to fit him above an inclined zigzag line
beneath which bloomed an abstraction of flame.
The pictograph was captioned, "In case of fire use stairs."

So I stood there, having punched the button,
thinking up a few of the situations
in which that might not be the best advice.
A thin, soft edge of the urge to weep nudged
faintly in from somewhere, while the tilted man
seemed steadily to soldier on, embodying
cool-headed swift descent to safety and fresh air,
all confidence in his Grecian-urn immobility.
I could not shake the vision of his pitching
forward onto his blunt-ended arms, his legs,
one almost a foot shorter than the other,
waving dimly in the smoke-thickened air
like a pair of broken scissors, as the flames
break through from below and start to climb the walls.

Goodbye

Hard words endure, but more
and more they sift and separate

like vapor into clouds of images—
sunlight on a handsbreadth purl

in the midst of a rocky trickle
a boy could bestride, a broken

hay baler slowly becoming
part of a weedy hill, the scratch

and knock of a head of orchard grass
at the wide crack between two boards

in the wall of a corncrib—
that stay when the words are gone.

For William Matthews

1942–1997

If nothing ever happens more than once,
we still think we know enough to entitle us
to a few expectations, and to love

those moments when anticipated pleasures
strike us sweetly numb. How many times
you felt and spoke the exact way it was

to be in a room where musicians worked
toward those rare and swiftly fleeting
convergences of everything there is,

the world honed down to what vibrated
between your glass and the cone of light
in smoky air where sorcery kicked in

often enough to keep you coming back.
One time in Washington, it was you
the light picked out at an elevated podium,

your head tilted a little to one side
as if you were listening and speaking at once,
eyes sometimes closed, the soft voice

grazing carefully over lines and sentences,
and it came to me that if I had the power
to keep you around and turn you off and on

at will, as if you were a radio,
I would have all I need of what I get
from writing poems, and could quit.

It might be so. Slavery's illegal,
and now you are gone. I still like telling it,
bringing back the realization of that moment

to meet the disbelief or faith it might arouse.
I believe it. Like the tunes you wrote about,
your poems don't so much bring back a time

as lift us out of this one toward another
that has never been, not yet, no matter
how hard we might wish it had been, however
much about it comes just close enough.

At the Thursday Night Jam, Remembering an Absent Singer

W. R. B., 1915–1995

Suppose he held some notes the rest of us
never quite caught, exactly, for all his singing,
the old LPs, sheet music by the ream,
the plunder of an aging amateur;
still, every now and then he nailed it hard:
a bar or two would ride the stricken air
and lift us to a treasured patch of grief.
A mountain's shadow at sunup, sliding down
a slope on its western side, the small clear gap
above a smokestack before the vapor clouds,
could hold us weightless in a mellow tone.

Some couples, when they dance, are dancing now
and dancing years ago, lifetimes honed to this.
Musicians, watching, lean closer together
and work a little tighter, thinking back
to their own favorite brush with faultlessness.
On a salt-specked wharf one August, late sunlight
was ricocheting off the brass and wood
and acrobatic fingers over keys;
the music rose so far into the world
that even deadpan gulls swayed as it swayed,
and we were all just lucky so-and-sos.

On certain evenings since his last sweet session
the troubles on our minds make way for songs
it's hard to hear in any voice but his,
and now, as dusk leans in and lights come on,
an old friend starts to tune an upright bass,
a muted trumpet tests the atmosphere.

Desert Passage

They built this road for travel, not for stopping;
the emptiness has features, but they pass.
The land invites a glance around for windmills,
while a voice asks, “Is there water under here?”

All day I’ve seen things flapping in the wind—
a fertilizer bag caught in a fence,
a pair of shoes on an electric wire,
shreds of stars and stripes tied to a bamboo pole.

Off to the right, a car with its hood up,
nobody anywhere in sight of it,
makes me sag inside a little, bringing back
or almost back a time I may have passed

that haunts me when I see abandoned cars.
Toward dusk a temporary roadside sign
blown off its tripod, face down on the shoulder,
whispers its dire announcement to the ground.

In the Galisteo Basin

Cresting a rise a mile and a half from home, we drop
into the fringes of the Galisteo Watershed,
where these dry hills shed mostly shale and dust.

South of here the road to Albuquerque crosses
the Rio Galisteo itself. For two years
we have lived here, and in that time seen water

in the Rio Galisteo once, after a week of rain.
Most of the time, it is a river of sand, etched with rills
where water last went by, the sinuous bars aswirl

between the banks, dropped wherever the flow decreed.
Up closer, the dunelike surfaces are stippled with tracks of birds,
coyotes, and mule deer. Beyond the banks on either side,

broad flats extend toward steeper slopes
that water reaches once or twice in a hundred years.
Just east, the banks rise up to form Tom Payne Gulch,

about whose naming I have discovered nothing,
yet it brings to mind the Tom Payne I knew years ago,
and who, by forces known to those who like to claim

that there are no coincidences, worked with me to build
a driveway's crossing over a narrow trickle in a meadow
on my father's farm. His work was absorbing

to watch and to learn from, as he molded a place
off to one side of the stream in which to pour the concrete
for a low-water bridge with two culverts through it,

then moved the stream over to where the bridge was.
It seemed brilliant in the making, but it failed.
Water got under the slab, washed out the dirt beneath,

and the top proved too thin to keep from cracking under use.
With a rented jackhammer I broke up most of the bridge,
bought and placed a third and larger piece of culvert pipe,

bent and tied a few dozen feet of old silo hoop to form
a net of reinforcement for the top, and ordered the concrete
to be poured over it. At last I smoothed a small rectangle

in the top, off to one side, and twigged initials and a date into it.
I soon let go of cursing Tom Payne's work, and could enjoy
my having learned to make what I had made.

As decades passed, it got to where I went for years
without thinking about that episode, but here in this dry country
far from that little stream in Virginia whose annual flow

may well exceed what passes here, I think of it,
thanks to a small notch in a great landscape
whose name's origin, if lost, feels found to me.

Art and Life

In the Portland Museum of Art's snack bar
one July morning, a young woman worked
at the board that lists the specials of the day.
From her little stepladder she leaned in

with various colored chalks, using both point
and edge, adjusting with her fingertips,
experimenting with size and color, print
and script, once or twice stepping down and back,

then homing in on what was to be solved.
The whole thing might have taken her ten minutes.
At last she moved a little farther back
to see how what she'd done had changed the room,

while we, who had the good luck to be there
at the beginning of her day, beheld
the change she couldn't know that she had wrought
merely by how her red hair caught the light.

Yesterdays

for Jael McHenry

"Of all his whims," she said, "I think of one
least gratefully. He'd squint and hold up two
fingers and wave them back and forth just three
inches from my face. 'How many is it? Four?
Are you seeing double? What's half of five?
I hope you held off drinking until six.'

I hadn't had a drop to drink in six—
what? Months? Years? A unit of time is one
vast era or one second, and if I've
learned anything, it's that we needn't be too
particular. What's a fiction writer for?
To bait him once, I said, 'It looks like three,

but on that hand, the difference between three
and five is hard to spot, and being sick's
as easy for you as being well. Before
you take your hand away and claim you've won,
consider what your tricks have brought us to.
We toil in separate cells from nine to five,

and get our desks cleared on the stroke of five.
The elevator drops us twenty-three
stories, which is a lot more than the two
sad stories we drag into this house at six,
each of us ready to tell the other one
what our parents put us through when we were four.'

'How long,' he asked, 'with that shrink? Is it four
years now he's taught you confrontation? Five?
What difference does it make, if I'm the one
who gets it wrong? Would we add up to three
if we departed from the bitter basics
and counted the sane and nutty yous as two?'

'Put your hands down,' I said. 'The left one, too.
The ultimatum you've been pining for
will not arrive, though I'll be gone by six
tomorrow. I'll set the alarm for five.
I'll throw my things in the backs of two or three
friends' cars and split.' I look out for number one."

A day or two ago, starting at five,
I scribbled out four drafts, discarded three,
then six or half a dozen, and kept this one.

Chapel in the Air

On Friday nights the minister sat down
to write the sermon he would deliver live
and tape record for use on radio,
The Wireless Tabernacle, his own half hour.
All this was maybe fifty years ago
in a small town suburbs have since engulfed.
An engineer with snips and splicing tape
edited the recording, taking out
the sounds the preacher didn't want to make—
his voice's nervous tics, the grunts and coughs.

Later, on his own time, the engineer
gathered together all the excised noises
and spliced them to a reel he kept prepared
against a foreordained dawning of wrath,
incompetence, or moral turpitude.
That day he would broadcast the whole half hour
beginning, "Greetings from the Blessed Air!"
and passing on through every senseless sound
the preacher's rebellious tongue had brought him to—
erha burp snarf harrumph et cetera.

At last the engineer began to dream
of being fired, then sneaking back one night
into the studio to beam that reel
of nonsense to the world. He had his plan.
Years passed, the last show aired, the two men died.
The reel of tape is somewhere, though, and waits.
The syllables are in their sealed tin can
yearning to be unraveled through the ether
where they will lean and sway in harmony,
singe the frail ears of late-night listeners,
ripple the leaves of prayer books and Bibles,
and shake the hard foundations of the Word.

The Final Morbidity of the Interior Embezzler

> It may seem morbid of an embezzler to keep a memorandum,
> yet many of them do. It may be mere neatness.
> —Wallace Stevens, "Surety and Fidelity Claims"

I've made a little sluice-gate in the flow
of cash across the spreadsheet on my screen.
Amid torrential chaos and foreseen
disasters it maintains its small and slow
on-off diversions, so my work can show
the delicacy of difference between
the beans I count and one uncounted bean,
and where the latter might invisibly go.

The hollowed shoe tree, the hermetic jar
are gadgetry I might revert to yet.
There is the money of the thing, the far
secure retirement years, the deep-hedged bet,
but I love working where the unknowns are,
and writing down what I need to forget.

Not Quite Lost in Space

The gravel drive surrounds me as I stare
at the minuscule brightness of a grain
of quartzite on a stucco pilaster
bracing the coyote fence that ends our lane.

It caught the sun and aimed it at my eye.
How small a target can that slim ray find?
I shift my head from left to right and see
that maybe one square foot has been aligned

with me for several seconds in its turning
downward as the sun goes up. If I stood
just here at this time for a year of mornings,
would this convergence ever be renewed?

Spheres crowd my mind, vast diagrams, slow change
in annual cycles. I try to recall
the little I have learned about Stonehenge,
or when the moon shone down the upstairs hall.

Now as the seconds pass, the light goes out,
but for a while these ill-formed thoughts revolve.
I stand here coiled in orbits, head to foot,
because this tilted world is where I live.

A Single Shoe on a Single Horse

Milton J. Hawley, 1919–1980

I was nineteen, home for the summer, standing
in the stable with Mutt Hawley, the farrier
incumbent back then in our neighborhood,
a man a little under six feet tall
and a little under three hundred pounds.
A cigar stayed in his mouth most of the time,
and a small green sponge on an elastic band
around his head caught the sweat from his brow.
I held the horses as he worked his way
from one foot to the next—front, hind, hind, front—
pulling the old shoes off, trimming the hooves,
rasping them level, nailing new shoes on,
turning and tightening clinches, smoothing off.
I stood there learning how a trade like his
could hold infinities in a small space
where the same moves made many times a day
could show you something new at any moment.
Then, into that almost hypnotic blend
of hammer-stroke and hoof on concrete aisle,
dust in a shaft of light from a door ajar,
Mutt's question broke the air. He asked how close
I was to taking the Pony Club A tests.
I said I'd take them later that same summer.
"OK, then. Remember the Manual says
an A rider should know how to shoe a horse?"
I didn't remember, but I let that pass.
"I haven't read the whole thing, but somebody
showed me that part. Wanted to know what I thought."
        "Well, what did you think?"
                                "Looks all right on paper.
It could be tough to put it into practice,
but we have what we need here, and I think
maybe you ought to put just one shoe on.

If you want to. From now on you could say
you did that much."

I'd never driven one,
but I knew a mis-aimed nail could hurt a horse.

"What do you mean by what we need?"

"I mean
the next horse on my list is yours. He'll stand,
so we can take our time, and I can watch you
every second. You still might make mistakes,
but I think I can fix them if I have to.
I will not, *will not* let you hurt his foot."

"All right," I said, and turned to get the horse,
patting him as we walked to where Mutt stood.
He was removing his vast leather apron.

"Put this on," he said.

"For just one shoe? Really?"

"Damn right, really. He snatches that foot one time
with an unclinched nail in it, he'll show you
something there's no other way to find out.
Put it on." He blushed a little. "Just wrap
the thongs twice around your waist."

I did as told,
and then he had me pull the near front shoe.
I tried to make what moves I'd made before,
watching for things I'd do for the first time.
I trimmed the hoof and rasped it level, taking
what seemed five times as long as Mutt would have,
then took a little advice from him about
how near it was to being right, and rasped
one side a trifle more. My fear of mistakes
was easing off, and my horse's slow breathing
made him seem to be on the verge of sleep.
My back was stiffening and my neck was sweating,
as much from anxiety as from the heat.

"Go upstairs to the shop," Mutt said, "and grab
a short scrap of two-by."

He held it down
on the anvil and watched me drive some nails,
so I could learn how different they were,
the head off center, making one side flat
from head to point, the head itself in facets
like a crude jewel, the shaft frictionless,
designed to hold only when it is clinched.
Faced the right way, its beveled point would take
a curved path to the outside of the hoof;
faced wrong, the point turns inward, lames the horse.
The small light hammer took more wrist than arm,
but I began to feel how it should feel.
Back at the hoof, I held the shoe against it
and brought its edges near the hoof's outline,
then looked at Mutt, who nodded and said, "Nail."
It took a moment to see which hand did what
as they tried to hold the hoof, a nail, the shoe,
the hammer. Then came the sweet discovery
that after the first nail was driven tight
and its end wrung off, the shoe and the foot
were as one for the rest of the way. Mutt leaned
down close over each nail I drove, and twice
helped me start over. When all eight were in,
I pulled the foot forward to my aproned knee,
rasped a notch for each clinch, and struck them down.
Mutt pointed out that if I practiced more,
the row of clinches on each side of the hoof
would be a little straighter, but these would hold.
He handed me the rasp to smooth the toe
off even with the shoe. I let the foot
down to the floor, stood, and untied the apron.
I was still breathing hard, hoping my horse
would be all right. Mutt shook my hand and said,
"Good job. We got away with it."
My horse
stamped his shod hoof, and the clack on concrete

awakened centuries of horses racing,
pulling loads over stony fields, or clattering
in paved courtyards, richly caparisoned
or working in plain harness, striking sparks
from stones with the fresh iron on which they moved,
churning earth that lost nothing for want of a nail.

A Firm Stance on Level Ground

At a midpoint in the journey of our life
I drove into a small town on the Plains
beneath a sky like sheets of churning pewter,
and heard the siren. Its slow rise and fall
held steady from one place, like a firehouse horn.

Two men stood out in front of a liquor store,
so I pulled over, rolled my window down,
and said, "If you were strangers to these parts
and heard that siren when you came through here,
what would you do?" "It's a tornado warning."

"I thought it might be. So. What's your advice?"
"Where you headed?" "Wichita." "That's good.
The storm's behind you. I'd just keep on going."
What can we know? With faith more in the way
they stood than in what they said, I've driven on.

II

Crooked Run
(1996–2006)

This is the stream I can't set foot in twice,
however often it has drawn my steps
to thread known rocks and trees toward a place
where the sharp surge of recollection shapes
itself then fades, as brightness fades and drops
groundward when another day's work is done.
Holding to paths engraved on inward maps,
I hunt for ways, as I walk Crooked Run,
to bless these lands, these parents, that I have been their son.

Metes and Bounds

The land surveyor either sets or finds.
You read this in the markings on his plats:
at such-and-such a point a pipe is set,
at older corners planted stones are found.

Still, his is not the boundary that binds.
Wandering through my native hills and flats,
I see what fields are not encompassed yet,
how little time we have to hold our ground.

Creek Walk

In a single hour, between the banks of one small stream,
a heron takes an interrupted walk among crayfish
and frogs, each pause between strides frozen, like a picture,
each stride a slow transition from one stillness to the next.

Without knowing it, maybe, the frog awaits the beak
that strikes so quickly the frame around the picture
stretches out of shape, then snaps back.
The frog goes down the throat, wings lift and settle.

Now, as in ancient times, a beaver slips off the bank
and drops toward a point of buoyancy, his back and face
just out of water, legs moving as in a brisk walk,
the flat tail rowing up and down, leisure in every move.

Then simply gone, not there, as if a strong transparent hand
had lifted him, or shoved him under water—removed him,
anyway, to a place where he must somehow be needed.
Between those two, a sick raccoon is taking his final steps,

as if his illness were a brush-fire he could walk away from,
not rabies, bound to finish him in a day or two at most.
He came here, had his life, and as his last strength goes,
the little branch keeps washing over algae-laden stones.

Snapshots

Henry B. Taylor, 1873–1968

1

Out of communal silence the people
called Quakers have gathered to themselves
their quiet, steady way of being
in a world they choose not to reject.
In that context my grandfather Taylor thrived.
Presiding Clerk for almost forty years,
he had a gift for finding just the phrase
for rugged matters hard to bring to consensus.
At memorial meetings, especially,
he had a touch that came to be locally famous.
It got to where he was asked to speak
almost every time a Quaker died.
So, inevitably, came the death
of one for whom he had had little use.
An irreverent old rapscallion, he thought,
and tried to stay out of his way.
                                        The man's sons
came back to Goose Creek from distant homes
and found themselves a trifle out of their depth.
Taking advice, they asked Henry B.
to speak. He would have preferred not to,
but didn't see a way to turn them down.
Worked a day or two on a set of remarks
not without justice but sparing the whole truth,
and when the time came, spoke them. Afterwards,
the sons made known their disappointment. "We wanted
an honest-to-God eulogy," they said, and he,
"I'm sorry. You picked two of the wrong men."

2

His kindly cleanliness of speech,
his upright square dealing, became

community property, almost
proverbial. For his son, an example
awesome, if not impossible.

He set Joe Jackson to work one morning
cleaning off the asparagus patch.
Pretty soon Crave Tate came past,
watched a moment, and observed
that the boss didn't want asparagus
pulled out with the weeds.
It takes years to establish asparagus.
"He said to clean it off," Jackson
replied, "and that's what I'm doin.
Go on bout y'own business.
I know what the man told me."
Tate went on up to the house
seeking clarity and vindication,
and got both, in a voice
that carried across two fields:
"Hell, no!" Not too strong
by some standards, maybe, but
the teenaged boy who would
become my father, in which role
he would think of this moment often,
laughed.
                All but fell down
laughing, in an astonished
seizure of relief
that the old man had it in him,
laughed till he had no more breath for it.

3

He told me once about a time when silence
was the best response he had to what occurred.
He'd engaged a fellow from out Between the Hills

to caponize some young male chickens
before they could grow up into roosters.
A delicate skill, practiced even then by few.

As he worked along, the fellow mentioned
he'd just that morning been in Hamilton
at the home of Mr. Harrison Branch.
"Mr. Branch a mighty fine man," he said,
"but he's awful quare." Breath held,
a deft small finger-twitch, a chicken set aside.
"They tell me all them Quakers is quare."

4

"Just look at that old man!" cried Leon Grooms,
and we all did, as he took two quick steps
while looking upward to watch
the steep trajectory of a fresh egg
we had just found in the haymow,
reaching out toward where his shoe-tops would be
in another step and a half, letting
the egg fall easily into the soft cradle
he had made of his hands, straightening,
holding it up unbroken, a quick wave
of thanks, then turning back to the weeds
he'd been raking when the wagon passed
down the driveway with us on it, headed back
to the field for another load of hay.
Leon had stood up as we rolled by,
held up our find and called out, "Mr. Taylor,
got an egg for you!" "All right! Throw it here!"
"He mean what he says?" It was an uphill throw
from a moving wagon, not quite thirty yards.
"I never knew him not to," my father said,
and Leon settled back into his windup.

5

One afternoon he stood with A. M. Janney
on the porch of Janney's Store,
when down the single street came—so quietly!—
a funeral procession, fraught
with somewhat more than the usual pomp.
Asa Moore's stunning voice rang out:
"My goodness, Henry, those people
sure know how to wrap it up, don't they?
Makes our ways look kind of sparse.
Maybe we need a religion
that would take us out like that."
Grandpa said, "What's good enough
to live by is good enough to die by."

6

At eighty-five, interrupted.
A stroke melted
one side of his face
and stopped him from walking.
Voice thin but speech clear,
he called to me from his wheelchair
as I came into the room,
"Henry, they've got me under!
Yes sir, this time
they've got me under!"
Believing and not believing,
wanting, as always in his presence,
to do right, I made some lame reply.
Yet within months
he was doing a slow dance
with an aluminum walker;
later, two canes, then one.
Went back to gardening.

Nine years later my father
stopped by there on his way home

from an auction, and mentioned
having bought a harness-maker's bench.
"Let's have a look."

So my father brought it in to the porch,
and the old man got up, put a hand
on the two tall wood jaws
of the vise, walked all around the piece,
swung a leg over the seat and sat,
working the vise treadle with his foot.
"Just fine," he said, "just fine."
That night, in his sleep, he died.

7

When Henry B. Taylor had been dead
for at least twenty years,
I was in Janney's Store myself,
and Asa Moore said, for maybe
the thirtieth time in forty years,
that I could never hope to be
the man my grandfather was.

Correct. But I had come at last
to know I was not called
to be the man another man had been.
Should not have said so.
Asa Moore, I mostly think,
meant well. I mostly wish
I had, too.
                So he was right.

The Dining Room at Springdale

Walter M. W. Splawn, 1883–1963

The Springdale Country Inn is two driveways
down from mine, so I go by it often enough
that I need not think, each time I pass,
of all I saw there, or heard about. Through childhood
I was a regular guest in the dining room,
at the dark table with the umbrella-belled
Tiffany lamp looming just above it,
the dumbwaiter in the corner, a danger
and a mystery, the dark-finished sideboard opposite
double doors through which, from the hall, I could see
Granddaddy sitting at the head of the table,
his eyes often closed, and when open, not steady,
for it had been many years since he had seen
the last thing he saw, whatever that was.
He said once that in the course of his last operation,
during which, for some good reason, he was conscious,
he became aware of a bad moment—a sound, maybe,
of breath sharply indrawn toward the shape of a swear-word,
or only a sag in the room's energy—when
everyone there came to know he would not see again.

Still, he kept at most of what he had mastered.
You can read for yourself in a life of Sam Rayburn
how before he was Speaker he persuaded Roosevelt
to appoint Dr. Splawn to the Interstate Commerce Commission.
He knew his freight lines, by God. I used to read to him,
long incomprehensible pages of economics,
or a draft of his own history of the University of Texas,
of which he had briefly been president.
He would pay me a little something per hour,
for I had come early to the ability to enunciate
what I did not understand. That skill still helps me get by.

In that somewhat under-illuminated room we gathered
several times a year for Sunday dinner, or an annual holiday,
when cooking and serving became the responsibility
of Joe Trammel, a Black man with a deficient leg.
He had had polio. He got along by making sure
the bad leg's knee locked straight before he touched down.
He swung it forward from the hip, and his lower leg,
striking the end of its arc from the knee, gave
a small extra hitch to his uneven but durable stride.

I do not remember not knowing him.

One afternoon in the garden, when I was about three,
I squatted down in the path of his hoeing,
and the blade made its eager way toward me,
lifting the soil and slicing off weeds,
and I screamed, and he laughed.
Years later, as a crew of us ate lunch
and told stories, he said that ghosts won't hurt you,
but they sure-God make you hurt yourself.

When he worked the dinners at Springdale
there would come, sometimes, moments I can almost re-enter
of suspenseful silence so heavy I knew how it would feel
to crawl out from under it. I never could learn
what, dimly foreseen—by me only?—filled the room
with overwhelming expectation, as Joe Trammel
circled the table and extended a dish-bearing hand
into the space above each place setting.

As most of us do once in a while, Granddaddy
would pull away from the room around him
into brief reverie. Being blind, he had gotten
out of the habit of pretending to alert presence;
he might tilt his head, close his eyes, and snap
his jaw, and you knew that something not in the room
was going vigorously on in that capable head.

He rarely took as much as half a minute, then came back,
having missed, apparently, nothing at all.
One night a few years before I was born,
there assembled in that dining room several men,
mostly Texan, like Granddaddy, and mostly,
like him, occupied with matters in Washington.
Mr. Rayburn was there, maybe young Johnson,
and Vice President Garner—old Cactus Jack,
who lived almost to the end of his ninety-ninth year,
and got into a few books of quotations by doubting
that the office he held was worth a bucket of warm spit.

But there and then, a fine evening, fraught
with laughter and good talk, winding down
after dessert and liqueurs, two or three old boys
still trading wisecracks, and Granddaddy withdrew,
then emerged, and said, "I believe it's time
for my warm milk, Joe." Then thought of his guests.
"I beg your pardon. I take a glass of warm milk
at the end of the evening. Would anyone else care for one?"
Silence of unusual heft. "Mr. Garner?" "Shit, no!"
The dry Texas hills crackled in the voice and rang
like sand against the delicate stemware on the white cloth.
"It'll make me sick to watch you drink it!"

Reporting this to my father, Joe Trammel
reminded him that you ain't supposed to let on,
when you're serving, that you hear what gets said
to others than you. "Couldn't keep a straight face
to save my soul, Mr. Tom. I had to set down
that tray and come on away from there."

My grandfather had that place for thirty years,
maybe a little longer. It had been a girls' school,
and a makeshift Civil War hospital. Such
are the glories that decline, in these
enfeebled times, toward bed and breakfast.

John Nance Garner, at the end of his second term,
retired to his home in Uvalde, Texas,
and the rest of his long life stayed out of Washington.

A Little Respect

From the farm next door, long after midnight, there came
one day last year the bray of a jackass, an unholy sound
I had not heard for years; by now it is nearly as much
a part of the air around me as the sound of my breathing,
but that first note set me off, down the hill and across
the meadow and up the road, then one farm north,
where old Foster was still working when I was a boy.
He assembled for haying a crew young and old, Black and white,
in an era when some men might have sent separate
and possibly equal water cans to the field, but Foster
had one can, one dipper, with which each man took his turn,
swirling the last swallow, not taken, into a jeweled
arc as he passed the dipper on and let out a breath
through his cooled throat like a velvet shout, and turned to work.

Down toward the edge of the bottom, then back into the hill,
two thirds of the load on already, and the mules balked.
It is a term rarely used in connection with horses,
for instance, whose methods of subverting human wishes
might be called stopping, quitting, refusing, or pulling back.
They shift about, under duress, to avoid moving on.
Mules balk. They put all four hoofs in touch with a force
below the earth's surface, and enter into a state
of patient remoteness not unlike prayer, or trance;
their apparent indifference to shouts, jerks, and blows
can lead their oppressors to an unexamined belief
that what they are doing is no more cruel than beating a rug.

So with Foster and his men. As usual, they tired first,
stepped back to take breath and wipe brow, and the air
settled, in nearly-noon sunlight, toward perfect stillness,
a transparency dense enough to suspend a fleck of chaff
or the odd wisp of hay, drooping weightlessly from the load
like a fern in a glass paperweight. Decreasingly labored

the sound of their breathing, and abrupt the halted buzz
of a fly landing somewhere. On the off side, the slight creak
of a strap under strain.
                                        A boy spoke. Just a kid, a ward
of the county, sent out to this farm to be learning to work.
"Let me try," he said, and these grown men looked down
on this half-grown Black boy, then back at the team,
whose roots in the field were perceptibly deepening.
"What the hell," one of the men said, "he can't do no worse
than we done." So Foster stepped toward him, held out the lines.
The boy took them, made them right in his hands, stood
just to the near side of the rear of the team, and spoke
to the blindered heads. "Come up there, Mr. Mule."

First stillness, then a calm, slow lean into the collars,
a hoof lifted, and another, and they walked off
up the windrow as if bound for their hearts' desire.
The boy glanced back as he walked with them, and grinned.
"Call em Mister. It help sometime to talk to mules that way."

An Artist from Another Place

Arshile Gorky, 1904–1948

Of the places the stream flowed through, one kept the name.
In my childhood, the 1940s, Crooked Run Farm
was the domain of Commodore Magruder, who came here
from all over the world, I guess, and fell to farming
with an amateur gusto that fueled many an anecdote.
Every so often my father would take his phone call—
some question easy enough for a man who'd had practice.
Instructed, Magruder would sometimes feel foolish.
"I might not know much about farming," he'd say,
"but by God, I could bring a battleship up Crooked Run."

His daughter, Agnes, lived off north, in Connecticut,
and came down with her family for the summer.
Her husband was Arshile Gorky, who stood once
just inside the door of the children's bedroom
in my parents' house, and looked, smiling, around
at the plaster walls that had been left unpapered
so my sister and I could use crayons on them. Just one
crayon past our doorsill, and that would be that,
but this side of it, we did whatever was within
the scope of our negligible skill, our small size.
This stranger, then, whose two daughters we were learning
to "have over," looked out from under dark eyebrows,
spoke through his mustache, his Armenian youth,
saying "Bot! This is what I try to do!"
                                                            Later on—
that same day? That same summer?—out in the yard
by the sandbox, Gorky stood at his easel, staring
at a space between trees, while his wife said "crayons"
so it sounded almost like "crowns," and explained his work.

A man like that living in our sort of country
could hardly keep from drawing attention—tall,

a touch on the shaggy side, sometimes unshod,
striding around on hilltops and by streams with a bundle
of crayons and a big tablet, making drawings
that could now account for nearly three hundred entries
in a *catalogue raisonné.*

The end
is there to read about. Car wreck, partial
paralysis, weeks of walking around in Connecticut,
hanging a trial noose on this branch or that,
Agnes sending the little girls out to play with him,
knowing he wouldn't do it if they were there watching.
The work and the stories endure. One time
Jim Cole, native farmer of few words, strong opinions,
drove in to the farm, needing to take up something—
wandering livestock, probably—with the Commodore,
but found no one at home and was starting away
when Gorky came out of the barn where he worked,
and, spying the critic he had just felt the need of,
seized Cole by the arm and escorted him into the studio.
There stood a big oil, maybe part of the *Calendar* series.
Whatever it was, Jim Cole failed to perceive in it
accurate depiction of anything he'd ever seen,
so stood there in silence until Gorky pressed him
for a response, then said, "Waal. Flashy, ain't it."
For that story's survival we have the artist to thank.

Every once in a while, then, at the Modern, or the Met,
his weird simultaneity of hard edge and soft form
draws me back to those days by the sandbox; once,
the baby Natasha sat in grass with a ball,
striped translucent yellow and opaque red,
so the red cast a shadow across her arm,
and her big sister Maro, three, looking straight
into me as she held the handle of my toy wagon,
said, "I am going to take this wagon far away. And—"
here her chin crumpled slightly, but she held

her tears and went on, “I’m never going to bring it
back to you.” I didn’t know what to say; I was four,
and didn’t believe her. Off she went to the far edge
of the yard, where I can see her yet, walking along
the fence by the driveway. Doubtless she brought
the wagon back; yet more than fifty years later,
I’ve never seen past that moment of brave, purposeful trudging.

Vision at Woods' Edge

Just a glimpse, doubtless nowhere near accurate,
through train window into the New Jersey thicket
past which we plunged in our self-absorbed hurtling
out of countryside into the urban explosion,
a mere glimpse: Farmall tractor squat on flat tires,
maybe rusted in place, three-foot circular saw
blade and log table mounted in front, and there,
running almost halfway from the edge to the center,
a crack in the steel, its ragged progress stopped
at a hole drilled, no bigger around than a dime,
yet large enough, if I step closer and look through
with one eye, to open out until I can see
the hillside above Uncle Will Smith's, the autumn
coming on, the men gathered for a day in the woods.

You might find this hard to believe. Just listen.
Long hours and short money will pave a mean road.
They mounted that saw on the tractor and went
to the woodlot, set up in minutes, and worked
whole trees into firewood and mill logs,
two men at the saw hoisting crosscut limbs
to the bench and down onto the blade, a sharp whine
for each cut, the stove-lengths flung to one side.
At quitting time one day they noticed the crack
starting in from a notch between teeth, so took
the blade loose and brought it in to the shop.
There, next day in good light, laid it down
on the bed of the drill press and stopped the crack
with a hole right at the point where it ended.
Then back to the woods, reassembled the saw,
and proceeded as if nothing was wrong.

Stand now where Uncle Will's pasture was,
look around at the fresh crop of houses encroaching,

and imagine, without passing judgment,
what acquaintance with firewood they harbor.
Where farm women toiled, soccer moms pool their cars,
and the skin of a pork loin is clear plastic.
Off there at woods' edge, where the trees have come over
the old barbed-wire fence, see the dead tractor,
saw-table in place but the blade not all there,
a piece taken out of it like a generous slice
from a pie. Look briefly, but look: they say
that when that one section spun loose it halved
a man's head as if it had been a melon,
laid it open like an anatomy textbook.
The stillness around the machine was not yet
what it is now, even after one man stepped back
to the switch and cut off the engine.
Just an eyeblink later, the abandoned tractor,
not quite vanished into this untended border,
is lifting the saw in the prayerful attitude
of a mantis, rigid enough to stop looking alive.

A Trace of Old Road Work

There was a time this road was narrower,
the blind curve sharper. In due course the state
was moved by equal parts of fact and fear
to smooth the curve with drill and dynamite.

One drill bit sank too deep into the rock
to be withdrawn, so they left it behind,
a pointing finger raised as if to mock
this stone-exploding urge in humankind.

When honeysuckle clambered to reclaim
the fresh-cut bank, vines covered up the drill.
A monument to nothing with a name,
it stands where I can show it to you still.

A Crosstown Breeze

A drift of wind
when August wheeled
brought back to mind
an alfalfa field

where green windrows
bleached down to hay
while storm clouds rose
and rolled our way.

With lighthearted strain
in our pastoral agon
we raced the rain
with baler and wagon,

driving each other
to hold the turn
out of the weather
and into the barn.

A nostalgic pause
claims we saved it all,
but I've known the loss
of the lifelong haul;

now gray concrete
and electric light
wear on my feet
and dull my sight.

So I keep asking,
as I stand here,
my cheek still basking
in that trick of air,

would I live that life
if I had the chance,
or is it enough
to have been there once?

My Dear Sister Hannah,

Carrie Taylor to Hannah Stabler
Our Distressed Home. Twelfth Month 3, 1864

It is clearer than ever now, we live
in the land of rebeldom,
and we wait, after three shocking days,
for what is yet to come.

We still have our roof above our heads,
but every day have feared
we should not have it very long.
Last Fourth Day night came word

that the Yankees were coming, burning up
everything in their way.
We trembled, yet could not quite believe
what we heard people say,

but next morning we heard it all again
and then caught sight of smoke
rising from stock pens, barns and fields
wherever we might look.

It was too true. They had come to burn
all but the dwelling houses,
and a few of those were so close to barns
as to be among the losses.

Smoke from haystacks in the fields
was pouring up all around;
Uncle Bernard's and Mrs. Heaton's barns
were burned right to the ground.

Such dreadful work was going on!
We put the boys on guard
to let us know when they saw the troops,
then Alice and I worked hard

at packing, for we were sure the house
        would go if they burned the barn.
Our nerves were stretched so tight we scarcely
        could guess which way to turn,

but at last we got our clothes together
        and more or less packed up,
then the soldiers passed by all around us
        and that day, did not stop.

It was said they had gone to Washington.
        We felt unsafe all the same,
and sure enough, next day, Sixth Day,
        about one o'clock, they came.

They rode up to the house by the dozen;
        our feelings were past description.
When at last we went out to talk to them
        they said they meant conscription

of all our horses, but we pled with them
        till they said they would leave one
besides the blind mare. Then they rode off,
        but another gang of them soon

swept down on us and took away
        the one horse that could see,
and set to driving off our stock
        despite all we could say—

the cows and sheep, even the calves.
        The burning party was stalled
a short way back, they said, and soon
        every corn-shock in the field

was hidden in thick smoke, from which
        small bursts of flame shot through.
One soldier rode round surveying the barn,
        to find which corner would do,

I suppose; we all went over to him,
entirely forgetting our fear,
and begged him not to start the fire,
and told him an officer

had already said they would burn no more,
that we could keep our barn.
He said, "Ladies, I am an officer,
and my orders are to burn."

William joined in the begging, too,
but had so little hope
of its doing any good at all
that he nearly gave it up,

but Alice and I got around him
and begged, and almost cried,
as if we were begging for our lives.
He asked to look inside,

then said, when he saw the flour kegs,
"Ladies, it has to go."
Those words renewed our energy,
and we implored as though

our hearts were near to breaking. Alice
was brushing tears away.
Though I could not quite squeeze out tears,
what all did we not say?

He looked irresolute for a while,
as if he might have a heart,
then "I cannot burn it" said at last,
rode a short way apart,

ordered his men to mount their horses,
then led them from where they stood
all crowded around the kitchen door,
hoping to rustle some food.

They took the saddle William had bought
since the beginning of the war,
but oh, we were thankful they left the barn.
Next day, another scare

came with the Yankees back down the pike
just as a strong wind blew
straight from the barn toward the house.
If the barn were burned, we knew

the house would surely go up with it;
but they proved a small force
just riding by, not doing any mischief.
William, without his horse,

had gone to herd up stock, while we
prepared to leave the house,
the dry goods packed as best we could,
the parlor carpet loose.

From us they took two dozen sheep,
four cows—indeed, all our stock,
and I believe nearly half our corn
burned standing in the shock.

They took our axe and butcher knives,
even the carriage whip,
&c., &c. They left the barn,
a miraculous escape,

yet we were broken as poor as poverty,
and the whole neighborhood
is full of destruction. Everything
that Uncle Bernard had

in his barn—wagon, implements
of all kinds, his good sleigh—
all was burned up, and their house, too,
did catch on fire, so they

carried most of the things out of it,
        but their servant girl climbed straight
to the garret window and threw water down
        on the roof and put it out.

They took Uncle Bernard's cows and sheep,
        even his watch. They are stripped.
Richard Henry's barn is gone, and Uncle
        Yardley's—although he kept

some nursery, so I hear—Tom Smith's,
        Will Smith's, out on the turn,
Sam Brown's, where Thomas Nichols lived,
        and nearly every barn

in this part of the country, most all
        the sheep and cows, complete
herds driven off, most of the horses,
        great quantities of the wheat,

corn and hay burned, Asa Janney's mill,
        and Watson's, where our wheat was.
Newton Taylor's mill is not burned yet.
        The only nearby house

to burn was Israel Young's. The worst
        destruction, we have found,
is among the unionists, but why
        has yet to be explained.

Second Day morning. I am ashamed
        to write so bad a letter,
but time is too scarce to write it over,
        and I might not do it better,

for the subject makes me so nervous
        I can hardly write.
Since I began this, another loss
        struck us Seventh Day night,

when our good blind mare died suddenly.
        William had ridden her
a day or two. She had the colic,
        he thinks. One thing is sure,

he has lost his last horse, poor man.
        He is down to one colt now.
One of our cows came home this morning—
        mine. Alice's pretty cow

is gone. Whole flocks and herds are loose
        along the mountain road,
and people are busily taking them up
        by stealth and force and fraud.

We have hogs, and would butcher tomorrow,
        but there is still the threat
of soldiers returning, for we have heard
        they are not done with us yet.

I despise the rebels more than ever
        for causing this awful mess.
Some weak-minded people will perhaps
        be more [*illegible*] after this,

but all I can say is they never had
        any unionism about them.
True, these were Sheridan's orders and men,
        though we could have done without them.

Alice thinks it would be nice to have
        a photograph of us
around the officer, pleading for the barn,
        but we looked so dolorous

I doubt we would gladly send it to you.
        William says ask Robert
if there is an old blind horse about
        he could trade for a bare cupboard.

I don't feel like starting over here,
but if we went away
we would be beggars. Uncle Henry
still has his barn today,

Uncle Aquilla's is not burned either,
so close to the house they spared it,
and Jonah Hatcher's is not; he bought
them off, as I have heard it.

I must close. How I wish to see thee!
Alice has much to tell,
and would write, but is too near crazy.
Do write us. Love to all.

Sincerely thy sister.

After High Water

We park the car,
pick our way over washed-out stone
to the bridge, and stare
at what can be wrought in a single afternoon.

The air is wholly calm;
gnats drift unbuffeted between here where we stand
and the almost motionless surface film
above the minnows. Lift your hand:

the point it marks in the sunlight represents
the level floodwaters reached in less
than half a day. To left and right the rusty pasture fence
is bearded with muddy grass,

except where it is broken
by the passage of a tree, or most of one. Today
sun burns, flat grass unbends, and minnows betoken
the seeming return of all that was swept away.

A Straight Stretch on the Far Side of Coolbrook

Henry S. Taylor, 1799–1866

From late childhood on, a fantasy I've kept
close to my chest is that I might meet old Henry S.,
at whose grave I've stood, in whose house often slept.
Neighboring Quakers made it their business,
when Coolbrook began to reveal what it would be,
to sit with him in inward inquiry whether less
of a house might better bespeak Friendly simplicity.
Who knows what that sober visitation wrought?
The rooms in silence hoard their deep posterity.

In the west gable date-stone, a year coarsely cut:
1827. Later descendants made
their own marks here, as postwar decades brought
fresh ways to pump household water upgrade,
or visions of a graceful first-floor bay window
at the front of the parlor, its foundation laid
in a hole dug at room's edge with shovel and hoe
by Edgar Brent, a Black man of kindly patience:
when my father, still in his high-chair, threw
his rattle so it landed by design or chance
in that pit at the parlor's brink, he would climb
out, toy in hand, and with minimal circumstance
place it on the high-chair tray. How much time
did Mr. Brent pass thus before I saw him myself,
gentle, distinguished, white-mustached, past prime,
dapper in straw Panama fresh from a clean shelf,
walking around Lincoln when I was just starting to?

I cast these lines back over the widening gulf
between now and then, when the farm was Henry B.'s, who
was the builder's grandson and grandfather to me.
I sat with him as he paged lovingly through
Henry S.'s day-book, teaching me to see

hints of the passions and tedium underlying life there
in decades before he had yet come to be.

Tucked in the book, a letter of late 1864
to a daughter away at school, about Union burning raids.
There are only copies now; the original is no more,
having failed to emerge from a senescent haze
in which my father unwittingly set it afloat
when he lent it to an enthusiast of local antiquities
whose mind was melting down, who simply forgot
he'd borrowed it, then died. We have the words,
the day-book bristles with that hand, smooth but taut,
and sometimes I almost believe, as I listen to birds
in old trees up the back meadow, that among them one
speaks for him. I turn toward the bridge whose last boards
barely cling to the beams, beyond it the road gone,
washed out, grown up in woods, so thoroughly effaced
that I can doubt it was ever there to drive on,
though I did that myself in a life long since past.

From here some thirty rods downstream, the branch
runs straight as a canal. The meadow lying west
of the bank is marked with faint hummock and trench,
left when the man made up his mind, somewhere
around 1840, to straighten that one stretch
of Crooked Run and shove it all over there
to the base of the far hill pasture. I glance back
at a picture on my wall, some years post-Daguerre,
small enough to cover with thumb, but no slack
in that tension of straight gaze, set lips, tight jaw.
A few hired men armed with shovel and pick,
a team of oxen, were all he required to draw
this landscape according to his will. At the end
of the Civil War he said he favored a law
that Secesh be deprived of the vote and bound
for life to the use of iron spoons. He was apt
to know what to think of my wish to shake his hand.

George Washington's Farewell to His Hounds

Some pillars of the Loudoun Hunt were gathered
to observe Tom Taylor's eighty-fifth birthday.
The weather on this last day of October
was warm enough to let us sit outside
where the sun was deepening its southward slant.
After a pause between stories trotted out

one after another, names of men and horses,
Joe Rogers recalled reading in the journals
of George Washington about the day his hounds
left Mount Vernon for good. He'd just about
hung up his tack; someone in Maryland
had bought the hounds, so he called them together

and rode up through the woods to the ferry
below Alexandria, put the pack aboard,
and sat astride his horse on the riverbank
while the hound-laden ferry pulled for the other shore.
Behind Joe Rogers's head, on the white brick wall,
a flake of paint had lifted, and it threw

a longer shadow in the steep sunlight
than you would expect from so small a thing.
It moved minutely upward while Joe Rogers
looked off toward the nearest hill and said,
"I can't help thinking he must have cast those hounds
a few times on his way up to the ferry.

Start one more fox." He kept himself from weeping.
"I wasn't there, but that's the way I see it."
A horse moved step by step along the hill,
nibbling the fading grass, and gave no thought
to history. The rest of us sat a while,
watching the evening drop a little deeper.

The Hayfork

I could get up from this kitchen table, I think,
and go see for myself whether, even now,
in the worn planks of the old barn floor,
there might still be two holes I saw made there
forty years ago, in a single second along
the ponderous time line of farming. Well,

I might get over there one of these days.
Meanwhile, what can I see from here? We entered
the barn's second story through a big sliding door
at the top of an earthen ramp. There was a haymow
on either side of a wagon-wide aisleway.
A rail hung from the ridgepole ran gable to gable.

High in a dark far end, when I was a boy,
the old hayfork still hung there, barely visible
in cobwebs and thin strips of sunlight
that burst between weathering boards. Shaped
like a three-foot inverted U, a giant staple,
it rusted toward absolute darkness against which

stark blobs left by last season's mud wasps
stood out like white spots on a heifer.
Who knew how long it had been there? Loose hay
was giving way to bales before I was born,
though here and there I've seen it made, the teams
of work-horses pulling the loader and wagon,

a man with a pitchfork working everyday magic
on top of the rack, the slow ride to the barn,
drawing the load up under the rail and the trip-stop.
A man dragged the fork down, hauling against
the tow-rope's weight the forty pounds of steel
with two barbed ends that grabbed the wads of hay.

Then the team, unhitched from the wagon, pulled
on the tow-rope, moving away from the barn,
lifting the hay toward the roof. A click
as the trolley-hook caught, then the hay
rode back along the rail into the mow
where men forked it away for the winter.

So to a day when I was twelve or thirteen,
when the baled hay we were making was plentiful,
stacked in the mow almost up to the roof,
and we were standing around in the aisleway
after the wagon backed out, catching breath,
getting ready to go back to the field. One man

up in the mow took a notion and snatched
at the tag-end of rope still fastened to the hayfork,
so it whirred down the track to a place just above
the middle of the aisleway, hit the trip, and dropped,
all faster, it seemed, than the noise of the track
could make us look up, and plunged its two points

into the floor just beside the left foot of Joe Trammel,
who stood there, leaning away from it, looking down
and then up, and around at all of us, a barnful
of men struck reverently silent in the presence
of whatever it was, the good luck that kept Joe
from injury, the bad luck that gave him his worst scare

in years, the innocent thoughtlessness that led
to that yank on the rope, the way things can go
for years without happening, biding their time
in a dust-whirling, cobwebby barn I can see
and smell and hear right now, staring down
at the grain in the wood of this kitchen table.

A Set of Hoofprints

A horse left this track as he walked.
Here a fore hoof made its print,
obscured as if by superscript
when hind came down where fore had been.
He turns toward home, extends his walk
till hind far overreaches fore
and every hoofprint is distinct.
You stand remembering how it felt
to sit those homeward-swinging strides,
to draw up by the darkening barn
and let your own feet touch the ground.

Valentine's Daffodils

I've stopped us here, my love,
upstream from Coolbrook, where the gravel road drops down
between two hills that bear faint surface marks,
the evidence of almost vanished lives.
Just on the south side of the road
locust and honeysuckle

roil over man-made shapes,
all that there is of Richard Henry Taylor's foundry,
where he cast farm bells, bullfrog-shaped doorstops,
and a one-horse plow of his own design.
Sometime in the 1870s
he went broke, sold out,

and moved to Delaware.
Across the road, beside this branch of Crooked Run,
a cluster of shred-petalled daffodils
comes bravely up each spring, out in that field.
I don't know yet what they have to do
with us, but there they are.

In 1890 the land
belonged to my great-grandfather, who sold it then
to William Valentine. The small log house
was probably in place before that time.
Though I have found several of them
in my family tree,

I'm no land surveyor;
still, one afternoon I drew a plat from the deed,
came out here with the sketch, and paced it off.
A rough idea, at least. On the west side
a short two-sided spur stuck out,
and where it ought to be

I saw five walnut trees
I've passed for years without a glance, lined up along
the northern edge of that small triangle.
You know me well enough to understand
the way that sudden rightness struck,
then settled into me.

I stood at the back line
looking downhill toward the daffodils, then stepped
lightly over to where the house may have been,
sat down between two rows of new corn,
and tried to wake my nerves toward
feeling the very spot

where earth's energy spikes
out of a household's ashes deep under plowed ground.
Well. William Valentine—called Uncle Billy
in a weird southern likeness of respect—
died in 1918. I have stood
by his stone in the Black

graveyard. His heirs allowed
someone else to occupy the rickety cabin—
a squatter whose name just would not quite come back
to the minds of a couple of old men
who did recall, before they died,
the man's dramatic end.

This was some years after
he had littered the place with odd chunks of old iron,
the kind of scrap they would have melted down
across the road, if the foundry hadn't failed.
A sharp axe head amidst it cut,
one morning of snowfall,

the hoof of a loose horse
that crossed the road to the south hill, leaving a mile
of crimson tracks before it could be caught.

The man himself, whoever he might have been,
came one night in his two-horse rig
down past the Chappelle place,

the horses running away,
and didn't quite make the hard curve past the bridge.
Chances are it was the crash that killed him,
battering him as it did pretty thoroughly
into a tree. All the same,
some people thought it odd

how cleanly his throat was slit,
and would not stop believing someone had cut him
before the horses ran off, but nobody
was able to say how. He was the last
of the cabin's human occupants,
though various animals

soon came to shelter there,
and they included a mongrel chicken-eating dog
whose owner's rifle shot had failed to kill him.
He fled here, the owner close behind him, and turned
in the cellar to flash two eyes
between which the man tried

putting a single bullet.
To spite hell the dog recovered, and moved on somewhere
a little more hospitable and forgiving,
but still clouds thoughts of the cabin with regret.
In 1935 Valentine's heirs
sold the place back to Taylors—

my grandfather this time.
An aerial photograph taken two years later—
probably as part of some New Deal project—
shows the lopsided yard along the edge
of the field; a dark patch within it
may be the house, or only

a charred spot on fresh earth
where the house had been. Either way, my father was there
when they took down what they could, burned the rest,
and worked things over with a bulldozer
to give the place back to the field.
That's what I know, sweetheart.

We glance from that small rise
to the swale beside the flowers, guessing where the house
could possibly have been. All that went on here,
the wanting and having and going without,
the passion or contented calm
of every spoken word,

the pitiful belongings,
the names themselves: obliterated, all gone away,
and I feel now with the force of quick wings
booming out overhead from a low-hanging limb
that what I want is you safe from harm
and these flowers to hold us to that.

Aka Fawn Meadow

> SPAM-2004-042 Application name: Hamilton Ridge aka Fawn Meadow. Project location: intersection of Sands Road (Route 709) with Taylor Road (Route 726). Request approval of Site Plan Amendment (SPAM) for a temporary sales trailer on lot 9.
>
> —Loudoun County land development applications accepted as of 5/29/04

At the county seat a map goes on display
to show the more than sixty lots these fields
have yielded to the husbandry of our day.
Until a wall of copper roofs unfolds

you might have time to catch a sunset's flare
beyond the trees along the old railroad—
not that there ever was a train through here.
Before the Civil War, bright prospects showed

a way to Harpers Ferry and beyond,
where West Virginia waited in its hills.
Though it bankrupted them, men shaped the ground
into a modest stretch of cuts and fills

that became a dump for agricultural scrap.
Now one of the streets carved on the stubbly fallow
is named for the railroad spur: Manassas Gap.
Alfalfa Court convenes across the hollow

to summon up the farm's last load of hay.
We find old words to call these new works by,
as if to name what goes could make it stay.
When mercury lamps wash out the Midnight Sky

and in Wooded Glen the bulldozed maples wilt,
settlers will ply the chemistry of the lawn
and high-priced rubber graze the fresh asphalt
beneath which lies the Meadow of the Fawn.

Boy Hunting in Bog

Joseph P. Taylor, 1913–1926

Through a window before which I've sat
often enough to take it wherever I go,
I watch, down there in the boggy section
of the meadow across the lane,

no one I can actually see, as he stalks,
feet bare, pants rolled above knees,
in one hand a thin staff with which
he prods the mud just ahead of him,

hunting snapping turtles. That is the truth.
One crunch of its jaw could amputate
the largest of his toes, but he handles the probe
with a safecracker's patience and nerve.

This is a boy who once looked out
from a photograph hung on a wall
of his old room in my grandparents' house
and surprised me—I was eight—by looking like me.

Now I sit here watching, and listen again
to my father's voice, stilled forever, telling
how his younger brother grew deeply
into a world with wild animals in it.

What goes on is that the stick in its prodding
strikes a changed texture, and Joe—that is his name—
knows he's got one, and slows down, feeling
with the stick for the head, then the tail.

Though the turtle is deep in that muck,
the boy finds it. His hand plunges down,
then tugs slowly. The turtle hangs there, its head
like an erect penis, enraged, snapping air.

Did experiment teach him? He just knows,
as he knows where the orphaned fox waits
for his gentle ministrations, or the snake.
But deep in his own brain, something else

bided its time, and made itself understood
too late. It was 1926. He was thirteen.
When, as they said, God had taken him,
my father said God could go to Hell.

The picture hangs now in a room
set aside for stored things, not people,
and sometimes I go there to see it,
but mostly I sit at the window

through which I can conjure that meadow,
and watch as the bare-legged boy
grabbles in watery mud for a creature
to which all need is basic and sudden:

kill, eat, lay eggs, settle down
in black mud, and bring darkness
up to the light when it rises to air
in the grip of a child who has left me

forever between where his photograph hangs
and the bog where I still see him walking
with a heron's slow stride, pure attention,
not quite of this world, but deep in it.

On the Air

The lay of this field's land is as it was
when nothing brought word faster than a horse,
but the plowman in his closed-cab tractor has
equipment tuned to an ethereal force.
He hears the news and watches actual weather.
Today the candidates quarrel over a war
one of them may have started, though the other
could have it on his hands within the year.

He thinks of a dark night on a long driveway
when across the band of light before his car
flashed a tremendous owl, about a yard
above the ground, its great wings heaving hard
to lift a rabbit large as itself to air
or else to fail. It was gone before he could say.

Hughesville Nights

> ὄρνυσθ᾽ οἵ καὶ τούτου ἀέθλου πειρήσεσθε.
> —*Iliad* 23.753

No one now alive, I think, was ever inside. The old store
collapsed into its own basement sometime around 1960,
having stood abandoned for close to a lifetime
there at the end of Bob Tiffany's driveway.
It was standing when I was in grade school;
I remember a low-hanging porch roof, a door
with an iron bar across it. All the wood
had gone gray, the paint disappeared, and the chimney
was starting to come apart at the top. Years later,
when I was living back there again, an indistinct heap
of crumpled roof and busted boards emerged
from thin spots in the briary overgrowth.
Locust trees grew from the cellar floor.

One thing that happened here, though,
probably in my grandfather's time, whenever
I think about it, makes me start putting the place back
together, making use of what materials I have.
A small
general store, mostly staple goods and work clothes,
in the back room slabs of cured pork hanging.
On one side of the room a wood or coal stove
surrounded by objects that might once have been chairs,
or only aspire to be—nail kegs, say, or apple boxes.
Across the room, on the left as you come in the door,
the cash drawer and iron safe behind the counter
of laminated walnut strips, oil-stained, dented,
and nicked. A low, weak place in the floor
where you stand to pay, or to have purchases
written down in the book.
There are nights
after closing when men sit around for a spell,

a few loungers not quite done with the day.
A couple of oil lamps get turned up just a hair.
Squeak of corncob in crockery jug-neck,
soft boom of palm striking the stopper,
smoke in an undulant layer about even
with the tops of their heads. Somebody tells
another joke. Amid the laughter a notion takes shape
apparently in the air itself. Without a word
one of the men there reaches over and grabs an ear of corn,
shells off a good handful of kernels, and lays them
end to end, just touching, in a row perpendicular
to the counter's front edge. There is joshing
and nudging about who will go first, then
a cheer as one man steps to the counter,
unbuttons his fly, makes ready the implement,
and with it sweeps aside that part of the row
he can thus reach.

By now the rest of the men
have arranged a rotation: each steps from the contest
into the committee of referees counting kernels
and calling out totals. Someone has the thought
to keep score on a slate, just a single initial
and a number. The row is rebuilt under watchful eyes.
One man sets a scale-weight down to mark a place,
another demands that two small kernels be thrown out.
The next man steps up, whips out and across,
takes the count. There are hoarse whoops
and high, loony giggles. "What color is that,
do you reckon?" "By God, you'd a got more
if you wadn't so crooked."

It ended somehow,
as such evenings do, in good humor or ill,
men stepping out into the night to sniff air
and make their various ways homeward over
the very hills and hollows I have lately been walking.
Among them there may have been a winner,
possibly more than one loser, but now,

however it was, there is nobody living
who could name a single one of them. The story
reached me as a curious example
of ingenuity in the use of shelled corn,
but soon enough the laughter dies down,
and it comes now to say that what matters most
about memory is what is forgotten forever.

Creek Walk

Strolling the banks of Crooked Run
I round a bend and happen on
a skeleton and rippling shreds
of bone-white skin in the oxbow pool.
It takes but a glance to identify
the stark remains of a tall foxhound
held in a nearly running posture
here at the end of a neighbor's pasture.
The open jaws might appear to say
we all must find our hard deathbeds,
but today I'm out to overrule
such hurts as I've been mastered by.
The earth's plain speech is all I've found:
no agony in the mouth stretched wide,
just water rinsing flesh away
and bones on their final seaward ride.

III

Understanding Fiction
(1986–1996)

Understanding Fiction

What brings it to mind this time? The decal
from East Stroudsburg State in the window
ahead of me as traffic winds to the airport?

Maybe we pass the Stroudwater Landing apartments.
Whatever it is, you who are with me get to hear it
all over again: how once, just out of college

or maybe a year or two later, into the first
teaching job, some circumstance found me
in the home of an old friend, one of the mentors

to whom I owe what I am, on one of those days
when the airwaves are filled with football.
We remember it now as four games, and swear

to one another, and to others, that this
is what happened. In the second game,
as men unpiled from a crowded scramble,

a calm voice remarked that Mike Stroud
had been in on the tackle, and we told
ourselves that we had heard the same thing

in the first game. Odd. So we listened,
or claimed to be listening, and drank,
and took what we were pleased to call notice.

Never an isolating or identifying shot,
just these brief observations of crowds:
Mike Stroud was in all four games.

An astonishing trick, a terrific story—
some plot of the color commentators,
a tribute to a friend with a birthday,

or maybe just a joke on the world.
I tell it at least four times a year,
and each time it is longer ago.

Mike Stroud, if he ever played football,
does not do so now, but he might
even have played only one game

that late fall day in—oh, 1967, let's say.
We were drinking. God knows what we heard.
But I tell it again, and see how

to help you believe it, so I make
some adjustment of voice or detail,
and the story strides into the future.

Frank Amos and the Way Things Work

My wife and I are standing in my sister's yard,
talking to the man who built our house,
across the field from here. He's retired now,

though he looks much as he did eight years ago,
when horses grazed our hill. But he's not well;
we've known for about a year. We ask him how it's going.

"Not too bad. They do this radiation"—
he pronounces the first *a* short—"every two weeks,
ten treatments. I've got these maps on my chest, see"—

he opens his shirt, and there the purple crosses
and rectangles are. "Got 'em like that on my back, too.
The lens that shoots the rays is up overhead,

and there's a big dish, like, underneath—maybe
to catch the rays after they've gone through me,
I don't know. The lens and dish are hung

to a big circular rack that they can rotate
around the table, so you don't have to move
when they want to shoot from the other side.

I told 'em today, my breast bone sticks out
too much or something, I can't lie down too long
on this hard table, so I'll just hold myself up

on my arms till you tell me I have to lie down
and hold still. Seemed to go all right.
I have to go all the way to Winchester

for the treatments—five minutes. Down here,
all they have is a CAT scan. Seen one of those?
You should. They run you through it and stop you

every inch or so, and it takes a picture
just like you'd been sliced in two. Cross section."
A grasshopper jumps against my leg; I think

of the day the framing got to where
he could see how the walls would be, and he said,
"God, this'll be a bitch of a drywall job."

He leans against the van, eyes bright, the last
two letters of his CB handle—GRAYBEARD—
emerging from behind him. "I don't know,

I just have a feeling, I think we're going
to come out of this all right." We pass the evening
talking over things you have to imagine

with your hands, taking turns with the pleasure
of being understood, touching on work in the West
Virginia coal mines, black blasting powder, the way

one man on a bridge-building crew would toss
hot rivets with a pair of tongs and the man
on the girder would catch them in this tin thing,

like a funnel, and then we get on carbide lanterns—
back to the mines—and from there to the old-time
gaslights fed by acetylene produced

in a carbide plant you built outside, just far
enough from the house, because every so often
a batch of carbide would explode, and you

didn't want anything like that in the cellar.
Better to have it off a little ways.
And all the time, part of me is watching him,

wondering how sick he is, thinking *This*
is the man who built our house. Finally
it's past suppertime, and he takes off.

We wish him the best, and send regards to Myrtle,
        and the old van backs into the turnaround
        and lurches toward the road. The rest of us

go inside to my sister's kitchen, and look out
        in time to see him coming back. He leans out his window.
        "Henry, I don't know why I didn't remember

till I got out to the road, but it's just come to me—
        the town lights over in Romney used to run
        on carbide, like we were talking about.

They had a big plant that put out enough gas
        to do all the streetlights. I just happened
        to remember that, and I thought you'd like to know."

Free Throw

for David Schiller

Hunched at a desk, my back to a window
    through which, if I turned around, I could see
    fields I used to cross daily on horseback,

having scribbled some lines toward what turns out
    to be nothing, I tear off a sheet and crush it
    into a ball. As my hand closes, David,

I see you in the open door of a van
    at a horse show twenty-five years ago;
    you came five Greyhound hours to see me there.

You hold a damp rubdown sponge on your fingers,
    watching a bucket as if it might move
    from where it sits on the trampled ground

ten yards away. Your wrist flicks twice, like
    the head of a snake striking, your arm flows
    over your free hand, the sponge arcs and drops

where you look. You do this again and again;
    I retrieve, wring out, toss, and you shoot
    as you did our last year at boarding school:

as if nothing else mattered. I am the willing
    ball boy, knowing that this is how it is
    when my horse canters down to a triple-bar.

Those were the actions we lived in then. Now,
    I spot the wastebasket in living-room clutter,
    partly obscured by the leaf of a table,

and my unthinking fingers begin to heft
    this wad of paper. I still ride once in a while,
    and you, these days, are running marathons,

so things are mostly not bad. But much that I once
intended to do shrinks now to this difficult,
trivial shot that no one will see.

It needs a high loft to clear the table-leaf
and drop straight down into the wastebasket.
More touch than eye, you might say.

I watch empty air for the flight path, my hand
flicks just out of my field of vision, thought stops,
and one more time, friend, it falls in.

An Instant on the Time Line

Do you remember, memory inquires,
what you were doing when Kennedy was shot?
The catastrophe-hardened heart replies,
Which one? Not that it matters: neither scene
replays as sharply as the first time I saw
a twist-top taken from a bottle of beer.
It was in Roanoke. I came home from work
to find the Friday bunch already at it.
One of the revelers—I know his name,
but these days who knows what it's safe to tell?—
reached in the cooler and brought up a beer,
and smartly wrung the cap from the foamy lip.
I stopped and stared. He didn't look that strong.
Presidents and rock stars come and go,
and that picture doesn't fade. It wasn't much,
but I stood there on the surface of the world,
feeling it as it made another turn.

Within a Stone's Throw of Greatness

Among the guests I talked to once
at a wedding in the late sixties—
back when the principals at such affairs
were my own friends, not my children's—
there was the father of the groom,
who turned out to be a vice president
with the Hartford Insurance Company.
It had been almost thirteen years
since the death of Wallace Stevens,
but I put the question anyway.

"Yeah. Yeah, I knew Wally.
I even know why you're asking.
I'm aware that he wrote poetry.
I never read any of it,
but I'll tell you this:
he was a hell of an underwriter."

After a Movie

The last small credits fade
as house lights rise. Dazed in that radiant instant
of transition, you dwindle through the lobby
and out to curbside, pulling on a glove
with the decisive competence
of the scarred detective

or his quarry. Scanning
the rainlit street for taxicabs, you visualize,
without looking, your image in the window
of the jeweler's shop, where white hands hover
above the string of luminous pearls
on a faceless velvet bust.

Someone across the street
enters a bar, leaving behind a charged vacancy
in which you cut to the dim booth inside,
where you are seated, glancing at the door.
You lift an eyebrow, recognizing
the unnamed colleague

who will conspire with you
against whatever the volatile script provides. . . .
A cab pulls up. You stoop into the dark
and settle toward a version of yourself.
Your profile cruises past the city
on a home-drifting stream

through whose surface, sometimes,
you glimpse the life between the streambed and the ripples,
as, when your gestures are your own again,
your fingers lift a cup beyond whose rim
a room bursts into clarity
and light falls on all things.

Night Search for Lost Dog

Not yet midnight, but late, and in through the window
the sound of a fox barking often and not far away
made me sit up and strain for something else, a clue
to the disappearance, two days before, of a silly old dog;

maybe they were out there in some kind of standoff.
High whining under the odd crystalline barking
made me think she was caught on the fence through the woods.
So up, into clothes, the hickory walking stick Larry Higgins

whittled for me, and I went out into the late winter night,
the sky high overcast and giving back from somewhere
more light than I would have believed possible this time
of night and year, easy walking down the hill to the woods,

and there it was again, out the driveway and off
to the left, where I went then, onto gravel and clay
packed almost to pavement, not hard to walk quietly,
and the drive stretched along through the trees

as it seems to have done once in an old illustration
in a book my grandparents had. It was something like that,
since the sight of it made me stop and go soft at the center
that a landscape so long gone could still be there

under my feet, winding out to the clearing
where the fox barked again, just there where the drive
comes out of the trees. Quicker then, still quiet,
I took one step at a time, stopping once at a sound,

a faint rhythmic thumping that turned out, probably,
to be a wrinkle in the nylon parka working against
my own pulse beating somewhere inside it, so I went on
to the big field on the right, past the woods,

to a place in the fence where the barbed wire
will hold a climber with a stout stick to prop him,
and the fox galloped freely away over the hill.
After a while it was just myself standing there,

hearing for the first time the racket from the house
on the opposite hill, young hounds maybe sensing
someone walking and climbing as quietly as his age
and a noisy down parka would allow, but not knowing,

maybe, that he was looking for a dog that was born here
and stayed for eleven years, learning little, but loved,
then one day was simply not there. No sign of a fight
or the hoped-for standoff with the fox, or a coon,

rabid or not, the thought of which had prompted the stick
now supporting two folded hands, my chin resting on them,
my eyes going in and out of focus on a world that right then
it was good, after all, to be in, mystified though I was, and sad.

A Voltage Spike

In a motel at the wavering boundary between
countryside and a town whose name I don't bother to recall,
I stare through a generous window toward a clearing

of some half a dozen acres, bordered in pine
and a few varieties of deciduous trees,
the farther ones scraggling above a darker band

of background—trees even farther away, or a low hill.
Brown grass and broomsedge almost conceal the clay.
In the foreground a buried-cable pedestal rises

like a steel mullein stalk beside a walnut tree.
As I relax my gaze to a passive blur, the trees
darken and close in around a passing thought,

and the empty field becomes the backdrop
for a daydream not quite willed, as from the woods
come several men in coveralls and stocking caps.

They carry clubs—of wood or metal, I can't be sure—
and move toward the center of the field.
With stolid care they set to killing one another:

the clubs rise and fall to a steady, thoughtful rhythm,
methodically cracking faces, bones, and skulls.
No one groans or shouts as the bodies drop;

even the sound of labored breathing is oddly faint.
I come to myself taking quick and shallow breaths,
my hands trying to crush the arms of the chair,

my eyes blinking to dissolve the savage tableau.
A light wind sways the broomsedge, and a flock
of starlings settles down like a cast of seeds.

An Ending

At opposite ends of many of their days
one of them tiptoed as the other slept,
since they were wedded to opposing ways
of keeping such appointments as they kept.
What came of all that care is hard to know;
gold foil and compass are quaint figures for
the wayward spirals of their to and fro.
They frayed beyond the grasp of metaphor,
but once at Coolbrook, letting landscapes pass,
he watched a ripple in the antique pane
divide a horse that cropped the orchard grass
beyond the post-and-rail along the lane.
Its two halves stayed in step through edgeless air,
then joined and kept on grazing, unaware.

At the Grave of E. A. Robinson

Decades of vague intention drifted by
before I brought small thanks for your large voice—
a bunch of hothouse blooms and Queen Anne's lace
and four lines from "The Man Against the Sky."
My poems, whatever they do, will not repay
the debt they owe to yours, so I let pass
a swift half hour, watching the wind distress
the fringes of my fragile, doomed bouquet.

I beg your pardon, sir. You understood
what use there is in standing here like this,
speaking to one who hears as well as stone;
yet though no answer comes, it does me good
to sound aloud, above your resting place,
hard accents I will carry to my own.

Afternoons with a Boomerang

An insect afternoon
of annoyance, discontent, the vain wish to be
far away, and I sit on the patio
staring at lawn, woods, receding green patches
with the impossible loveliness
of vanished children's books—

yet here it is around me,
consoling if not healing; I know no kinder place
in which to bear involuntary gloom.
Then across the patio comes a blur,
red shorts, legs, arms, three strides to grass
and I can focus now

on Richard, coming out
from under the weight of his own troubles, his hand
cocked, gripping a bright handmade boomerang
that now he throws, like a knife at a target.
For sixty instantaneous feet
it flies straight, then yanks left

and banks upward, tilting
into level flight, a spun, evanescent circle
back to the house, then toward another sweep
by the woods, flickering in and out of view
against backgrounds of sycamore
and maple, sky and grass—

a flutter of silence
to where he pirouettes, watching the cycle close
as the end of the spiral drops within reach
and he plucks it from air. Our separate woes
may not pass for more than a moment,
but this is the moment.

Not that he never misses:
the stick will spin too hard to be caught, or a stray
current of air from the woods grabs an edge,
or he has to look into the sun. Sometimes
the gravel driveway breaks his stride
over the dampening grass.

Twenty minutes, half an hour,
and his arm tires; still, it always feels like forever,
infinite small variations within
the aboriginal pattern, and I think
that whatever their use among hunters,
artists most deeply own

these physical mysteries
of getting a skill right, or nearly so, or, rarely,
of getting it wrong, the shout going up
at the botched release, the sharp smile of disgust
as the boomerang goes off course
and snags itself in a tree.

Error and correction,
flight and return, my son pulling hard as he can
toward making a life that is his, lifting
himself a little from his private griefs,
and me, for a while, out of mine—
and though the pain returns,

he gives, in fading light,
a look of birthright ease to a difficult thing.
Whatever unrolls on this spiral path,
lifelong though it may be, and hard, is worth no more,
in the end, than these crystal instants
of grace and lighthearted awe.

Popped Balloon

For two days, off and on, the little boy
inflated a balloon and let it go,
whooping as it careened with a Bronx cheer
to a corner of the room. Where, after a while,
he let it lie for another day or so.
Then found it, tried to blow it up, and stood
dead still when it exploded in his face.

He wept and banged his forehead with his hand
while I told him how balloons get old and tired
from all that getting fat and going thin.
No use explaining; he wanted to have it back.
There are others, I said. No, that one. More tears.
At last he huffed a desperate breath at it;
the air flapped loosely through the ragged end

and made a splattered moan like a ripped kazoo,
a ghastly, joyful noise that set him off
through the house again, amazed at what he'd found.
I cheered him on. How could I keep from thinking
of other things that weaken until they break,
and limp through the world, making their healing groans?
A few more breaths, and two decades are gone.

Now, here is this young man, becoming more
himself with every blessing, every wound.
Like any doting father, I have prayed,
but he already bears his share of scars,
and finds, in answer to my selfish hopes,
fresh uses for what's left of broken toys,
a keener ear for the joy in crippled songs.

Master of None

The plastic safety card
hangs from my hand unread as flight attendants launch
their deadpan puppet show; like a motel room,
this familiar strangeness soothes me into ease
at being nowhere in particular, relief
that it is too late now to make sure
I am on the right plane.

Out in the afternoon
at the taxiway's edge, men in hard hats are standing
around a backhoe. The purpose of their ditch
is invisible from here, but as it lengthens,
I see myself standing as they do, watching
hydraulic feet swing down and dig in
to steady the machine,

or the bucket pulling it forward,
as a man inches across a comic-strip desert.
Like something alive, it changes the ground
from which I will soon lift away; in the cab,
a man with knowledge I have coveted
sits touching controls and watching
what hands can make happen.

An old story comes back,
from wartime, when steel was scarce, and broken parts
of farm machines had to be put back together;
on such an errand, once, my father stood around
for half a day, waiting his turn with a welder.
To kill time, he wondered aloud
how hard welding was,

and the shop foreman said,
"That dumb son of a bitch out there learned to do it."
So, out of necessity, he mastered it,

and I watched him for years; now greed gnaws at me
whenever I watch some close work well done
and remember the shop foreman's line,
or mysteries I absorbed

from my life among horses,
who taught me, in their way, most of what I know now.
With less faith, I have acted in plays, taken up
trim carpentry, writing computer programs,
tuning Volkswagens . . . these sidelines and others
have drawn me toward mastery
approached, or barely imagined.

For the sake of odd skills
I have shirked the labors I live by, and pursued
one more curiosity for my collection, or puttered
awhile with an old one, thereby evading
the higher, more difficult arts, such as knowing
at sight the life-changing moment
when the right touch or word

might turn aside the rage
that careens through the house like electrical wind,
or when a hand, lightly placed on a child,
might wean him without force from the TV set
where, as long as the light of the world's last days
washes over us, we can believe
we will always be here.

What more will I try
before turning again toward making what peace I can
with the consequences of ignorant choices?
What can I know now, but ice clicking in plastic
at thirty thousand feet? So I daydream
of earth-moving competence, held in air
by the skilled hands of strangers.

IV

The Flying Change

(1974–1985)

Landscape with Tractor

How would it be if you took yourself off
to a house set well back from a dirt road,
with, say, three acres of grass bounded
by road, driveway, and vegetable garden?

Spring and summer you would mow the field,
not down to lawn, but with a bushhog,
every six weeks or so, just often enough
to give grass a chance, and keep weeds down.

And one day—call it August, hot, a storm
recently past, things green and growing a bit,
and you're mowing, with half your mind
on something you'd rather be doing, or did once.

Three rounds, and then on the straight
alongside the road, maybe three swaths in
from where you are now, you glimpse it. People
will toss all kinds of crap from their cars.

It's a clothing-store dummy, for God's sake.
Another two rounds, and you'll have to stop,
contend with it, at least pull it off to one side.
You keep going. Two rounds more, then down

off the tractor, and Christ! Not a dummy, a corpse.
The field tilts, whirls, then steadies as you run.
Telephone. Sirens. Two local doctors use pitchforks
to turn the body, some four days dead, and ripening.

And the cause of death no mystery: two bullet holes
in the breast of a well-dressed Black woman
in perhaps her mid-thirties. They wrap her,
take her away. You take the rest of the day off.

Next day, you go back to the field, having
to mow over the damp dent in the tall grass
where bluebottle flies are still swirling,
but the bushhog disperses them, and all traces.

Weeks pass. You hear at the post office
that no one comes forward to say who she was.
Brought out from the city, they guess, and dumped
like a bag of beer cans. She was someone,

and now is no one, buried or burned
or dissected; but gone. And I ask you
again, how would it be? To go on with your life,
putting gas in the tractor, keeping down thistles,

and seeing, each time you pass that spot,
the form in the grass, the bright yellow skirt,
black shoes, the thing not quite like a face
whose gaze blasted past you at nothing

when the doctors heaved her over? To wonder,
from now on, what dope deal, betrayal,
or innocent refusal, brought her here,
and to know she will stay in that field till you die?

Somewhere Along the Way

You lean on a wire fence, looking across
a field of grain with a man you have stopped
to ask for directions. You are not lost.
You stopped here only so you could take a moment
to see whatever this old farmer sees
who crumbles heads of wheat between his palms.

Rust is lifting the red paint from his barn roof,
and earth hardens over the sunken arc
of his mower's iron wheel. All his sons
have grown and moved away, and the old woman
keeps herself in the parlor where the light
is always too weak to make shadows. He sniffs

at the grain in his hand, and cocks an ear
toward a dry tree ringing with cicadas.
There are people dying today, he says,
that never died before. He lifts an arm
and points, saying what you already knew
about the way you are trying to go;

you nod and thank him, and think of going on,
but only after you have stood and listened
a little while longer to the soft click
of the swaying grain heads soon to be cut,
and the low voice, edged with dim prophecy,
that settles down around you like the dust.

As on a Darkling Plain

The years pile up, but there rides with you still,
across old fields to which you have come back
to invent your home and cultivate the knack
of dying slowly, to contest your will
toward getting death behind you, to find a hill
where you can stop and let the reins go slack
and parse the dark swerve of the zodiac,
a face whose eyes find ways to hold you still.

They hold you now. You turn the chestnut mare
toward the next hill darkening to the west
and stop again. The eyes will sometimes change,
but they ride with you, glimmering and vast
as the sweet country you lost once, somewhere
between the Blue Ridge and the Wasatch Range.

Getting Himself Together

after Baudelaire's "Recueillement"

He takes his pain to the woods, to settle down.
Wanting the dark, he shuts the cabin door
while the town he left lies buried in thick air
he once breathed freely, watching others drown.
Back there, they run like cattle down a chute
to low at those lascivious marquees
or slobber over rubber novelties;
so he carries his pain here to shake it out
away from them. On the gray planks upstairs
old calendars are curling up like scrolls
until all he can see is the painted scene
of a mermaid combing starfish from her hair,
or a flyspecked sunset. Toward midnight he unrolls
his sleeping bag and beds down with his pain.

More Than One Way

As to the cat itself, traditionalists tend
to start with a dead one. Take a sharp knife
and cut rings at all four ankles, then half-ring the tail

on the underside. Open the belly from crotch
to throat, and peel the skin from the hind legs.
Punch a small hole above each second joint,

between tendon and bone, for the ends
of a ten-inch gambrel stick, tapered
toward its tips like a sailplane's wings.

Hang the whole business on a peg, head down,
at eye level. With two oak dowels, form a makeshift vise
to grip the base of the tail: as you pull, the tailbone

slips free like a leg being drawn from a stocking.
Coax the skin from the torso, slicing the stretching white
web of mesentery. The head, if you decide to try it,

takes patience. Cut to the end of the lower jaw,
hook your fingers deep in the incision,
and push with your thumbs on the skull.

Cut off the nose button from underneath,
and it will stay with the skin; but whatever care you take,
there are two shapeless holes where the eyes used to be.

If that goes too slowly, give up on the tail;
just chop it off. Forget the gambrel stick;
place one foot on the rear paws and snatch upward,

lifting the whole hide as you might lift
a shirt from a child. You can even make
a quick slice around the middle and pull both ways

at once, if all you are after is what is inside.
Traditional methods, however gently applied
to even the strongest of living subjects,

have predictable results. Think back now
to childhood: how you hung from a bar
by your hands, curled up and dived between your arms

and down lightly to touch earth with your toes,
then twirled back. There were times, at that
instant of liftoff, when you could see yourself

as if part of you stood to one side watching.
In such moments of grace, a cat might come to a move it awaits,
the right sound or look of love, out of its skin by way

of its eyes or breath, to put all its lives in your hands.
But if this happens often, you will come to count on it,
and begin to take pride in what you are merely given.

Should such error overtake you, do two things:
dull your knife on oak for a gambrel stick,
then whet it on stone toward the genuine task.

Shapes, Vanishings

1

Down a street in the town where I went
to high school twenty-odd years ago, by doorways
and shadows that change with the times, I walked
past a woman at whose glance I almost stopped cold,
almost to speak, to remind her of who I had been—
but walked on, not being certain it was she,
not knowing what I might find to say.
It wasn't quite the face I remembered, the years
being what they are, and I could have been wrong.

2

But that feeling of being stopped cold, stopped dead,
will not leave me, and I hark back
to the thing I remember her for, though God knows
how I could remind her of it now.
Well, one afternoon when I was fifteen
I sat in her class. She leaned on her desk,
facing us, the blackboard behind her arrayed
with geometrical figures—triangle, square,
pentagon, hexagon, et cetera. She pointed
and named them. "The five-sided figure," she said,
"is a polygon." So far so good, but then when she said
"The six-sided one is a hexagon," I wanted things clear.
Three or more sides is *poly,* I knew, but five only
is *penta,* and said so; she denied it,
and I pressed the issue, I, with no grades
to speak of, a miserable average to stand on
with an Archimedean pole—no world to move,
either, just a fact to get straight, but she
would have none of it, saying at last, "Are you
contradicting me?"

3

A small thing to remember a teacher for. Since then,
I have thought about justice often enough
to have earned my uncertainty about what it is,
but one hard fact from that day has stayed with me:
If you're going to be a smartass, you have to be right,
and not just some of the time. "Are you
contradicting me?" she had said, and I stopped
breathing a moment, the burden of her words
pressing down through me hard and quick, the huge
weight of knowing I was right, and beaten. She
had me. "No, ma'am," I managed to say, wishing
I had the whole thing down on tape to play back
to the principal, wishing I were ten feet tall
and never mistaken, ever, about anything in this world,
wishing I were older, and long gone from there.

4

Now I am older, and long gone from there.
What sense in a grudge over something so small?
What use to forgive her for something
she wouldn't remember? Now students
face me as I stand at my desk, and the shoe
may yet find its way to the other foot,
if it hasn't already. I couldn't charge
thirty-five cents for all that I know
of geometry; what little I learned is gone now,
like a face looming up for a second out of years
that dissolve in the mind like a single summer.
Therefore,
if ever she almost stops me again,
I will walk on as I have done once already,
remembering how we failed each other,
knowing better than to blame anyone.

Heartburn

It is not middle age,
you tell yourself, getting up
from the table without breathing too deeply,
lest breath stir the fire in your gut;
it's not crotchety digestion
flaring up after years of eating incautiously.
You've burned like this after dinner
since you were seventeen years old,

when they stood you in front
of a screen in a dark room,
and two men in green coats watched as radio-
active chalk drink swirled in the faint
light that picked out their gray faces.
But the thing gets harder to live with, and you spend more
ill-tempered time, these days, clawing
in the dark room for the tail end

of the pack of Rolaids
that must be somewhere, in one
of the tweed coats, maybe, that haven't been worn
for months, and you picture yourself
in a pith helmet, hacking trails
to the heart of the treacherous closet.
So. Get up,
put on what comes to hand, and go
out, down the dark drive to the gate

where you lean and look out
over fields at the mountain
and beyond it to the soft dome of cloud-light
suspended above the city
some fifty miles away.

Not far,
yet as bright as it looms, you remember that right here
a black cow has been lying dead
for weeks at the foot of the bank

below the drive, having
fallen down into the stream
when a section of the stone culvert caved in,
and the rock that pins her is bound
to weigh over a ton, so she'll
be there, pulsating with maggots, drawing the local
vermin out of the woods, until
someday the bones are clean enough

to pick up and ponder.
Dark as it is, you walk down
to her now, catch a whiff of her, and for some
reason the moil in your stomach
subsides. It is only farm death,
the sound and smell you've known all your life.
Still, you indulge
for a few moments the notion
that one day you too might end up

with your head in a creek,
under a rock, crushed into
the earth you once found other ways of wishing
to merge with.
Listen. The night wind
is not strong, but now it catches
a dead leaf just right, whips it against a twig, making
it sound like a train in a dream,
clicking out some message in code,

as if such things could speak
to your heart; but that leaf is
as dead as the cow, and the cow is about

the deadest thing you can think of
in this vicinity. Turn, then,
and guess for a little while at the houselights tricked out
on the side of the mountain, where
people may be watching TV,

or thinking, as you do,
that the time may be coming
for some sort of change, and the thought fans the flame
in your belly, your grip tightens
on the rail of the gate.
Now tears,
as you look up at the sky, make the stars seem to speak
with more meaning than they possess,
and they say that whatever you

burn for—some plausible
answers to the momentous
questions you can't even think of, or only
an uncomplicated evening
in bed with someone you have no
true claim to—you almost had hold of it once, but now
you recall it imperfectly.
If you need a change, just stand here,

by God, and you'll get it.
So turn once again, back up
the driveway, thinking, as lately you've come to,
that you can still make a wrong step
on rough ground, in the dark, and not
quite cripple yourself. Porchlights, left on to show the way
home, shine right in your eyes, and you
can't see a thing, but you'll get there.

Taking to the Woods

Clearing brush away
is the mean part of working up firewood from these
cut-off treetops—a chaotic souvenir
of the doubtful covenant I made the day
I marked a dozen white oak trees
and sold them for veneer.

There might be more in this
of character or courage if it were need that drove
my weekly trials in this little wood,
but this is amateur thrift, a middle-class
labor as much for solitude
as for a well-stocked stove.

For more than safety's sake,
therefore, I take a break to light up and daydream,
and as the chainsaw ticks and cools, I smoke
my way back to an hour spent years ago,
when I knelt above a shallow stream—
the scanty overflow

from the springhouse at my back.
The ache of holding still dwindled away to less
than the absent-minded effort that has carved
these grooves between my eyebrows; on the surface
oarlocked water-striders swerved
above the scribbled black

shadows minnows made
on rippled mud below their bright formations,
and a dragonfly, the green-eyed snakedoctor
with wings out of old histories of aviation,
backed and filled down a stair of nectar-
scent toward a jewelweed

                  and struck a brittle stillness
like the spell the wood boss broke when he touched my hand
      as I stood absorbed in the loggers' technique:
      "Have you ever seen a big tree fall?" "Yes."
            "Good." Not the graceful faint we make
                  of tall trees in the mind,

                  but swift and shattering.
I counted the growth rings—one hundred sixty-four—
      and found where, fifty years ago, the wood
      drew in against the drought one narrow ring;
            I touched the band that marked the year
                  when I was born, then stood

                  and let them drop the rest.
This is everyday danger, mundane spectacle,
      spectacular and dangerous all the same.
      I hover between hope that it is practical
            to give young trees more light, and shame
                  at laying old trees waste,

                  then yank the starting cord
and turn to dropping stovewood from this chest-high limb,
      my touch light, leaving real work to the saw,
      my concentration thorough and ignored
            at once, lest the blade take on a whim
                  of its own; and I think how

                  our small towns have collected
in legend the curious deaths of ordinary men—
      as once, on a siding up the road from here,
      Jim Kaylor, if that was his name, directed
            the coupling of a single freight car
                  to the middle of a train—

                  an intricacy he knew
as most of us know how to shave, say, or shift gears.
      That day, he managed to be caught somehow,

and the couplings clicked inside him, just below
the ribcage, and he hung between cars
in odd silence as the crew

swarmed from the depot,
told each other to stand back, give him air, send
for the doctor, and he asked for a cigarette,
received it with steady fingers, smoked, and saw—
well, what could he have seen? The end
of a boxcar, the set

of a face in disbelief,
or something, in smoke shapes before him, that he kept
when he finished the cigarette, flicked it aside,
nodded, and, as the boxcars were slipped
apart, dropped with a sound of relief
to the crossties, and died.

Now I think hard for men
mangled by tractors and bulls, or crushed under trees
that fall to axe or chainsaw in their season,
and for myself, who for no particular reason
so far survive, to watch the woodlot ease
under the dark again,

withdraw into the mist
of my unfocused eyes, into my waiting stare
across bare trees that lift toward landscapes
through which snakedoctors may still wheel to rest,
then to walk home, behind the shapes
my breath ghosts in sharp air.

Tradition and the Individual Talent

An old-school foxhunter let it get around
that he hunted a deer-proof pack. Hard to believe:
foxhounds are born to run foxes, all right,
but you have to make them stay off rabbits,
housecats, chickens, etc. They learn to stop
when the hound-whip cracks. Deer scent, though,
is strong enough to put whips out of their minds.

So, somebody asked, how do you do it?
Take a bag of deer scent and a hound,
put them both in a fifty-five-gallon oil drum,
and roll it down a hill or a rocky road.
God almighty. You claim this really works?
Seems to. One thing I'll say's for damn sure:
they stay away from fifty-five-gallon drums.

Varieties of Religious Experience

This old day-worker, cleaning up
the grounds of an abandoned church,
getting ready to paint & put in glass,
said somebody from away from here
had bought it & was going to start
using it again. Well, it had been
a Methodist church, were these Methodists?
He believed it wasn't anybody like that,
no sir, he said; it is some of these
holy-sanctified God damn people.

Barbed Wire

One summer afternoon when nothing much
was happening, they were standing around
a tractor beside the barn while a horse
in the field poked his head between two strands
of the barbed-wire fence to get at the grass
along the lane, when it happened—something

they passed around the wood stove late at night
for years, but never could explain—someone
may have dropped a wrench into the toolbox
or made a sudden move, or merely thought
what might happen if the horse got scared, and
then he did get scared, jumped sideways and ran

down the fence line, leaving chunks of his throat
skin and hair on every barb for ten feet
before he pulled free and ran a short way
into the field, stopped and planted his hoofs
wide apart like a sawhorse, hung his head
down as if to watch his blood running out,

almost as if he were about to speak
to them, who almost thought he could regret
that he no longer had the strength to stand,
then shuddered to his knees, fell on his side,
and gave up breathing while the dripping wire
hummed like a bowstring in the splintered air.

The Muse Once More

I take the air, the sun,
my ease, letting things go for a while, as the dog
blunders from my feet to the curb and back.
The words in the book I am holding recede,
waver into illegibility; the air
trembles with jet planes, birds invade;
it is one of those days

when nothing at all
can go wrong. Across the way, I see my neighbor
lurching onto his lawn with some machine—
a rug shampooer? No, he straps a box
to his side, fastens earphones to his head,
and walks his lawn, sweeping before him
the sensitive disc

of a metal detector.
What in God's name is he looking for? It is ten-thirty;
he ought to be at work. But neither am I,
so I do not hail him. Back and forth,
back and forth he trudges over the spongy grass,
swinging the handle, his head cocked
for a signal whose meaning

I cannot guess. A lost
earring, perhaps, or the tap to the water meter;
no relics lie in this developed earth.
The sun moves higher overhead; he sweats,
walks on, and in my own head I begin
to carry that heavy intentness,
waiting for the whine

that will let me know
I have struck—what? The cars pass on their various
errands, snapping the asphalt bubbles,

and I doze here, dreaming that something lies
under a suburban lawn, waiting to change
  my life, to draw me away from what
    I chose too long ago

    to forsake it now,
on some journey out of legend, to smuggle across
  the world's best-guarded borders this token,
  whatever it is, that says *I have risked*
  my life for this moment; do not forget me.
    Whatever this makes me, accept it;
      by this let me be known.

    And my neighbor walks on,
hunting the emblem that will tell him who he is now
  or might once have become. I will not wait
  to watch him find it; let it be the lost
  treasure that turns his head on the pillow
    as he drifts, as I do, toward sleep,
      out of the life he has chosen.

Learning the Language

Tonight the windows hold
all light inside: they fold
it back on walls, and spill
gold over things that tell
us who we are. We hold
them in the corners of our eyes,
            playing a game
we have not tried to name:

half watched, half left alone,
the antique wood we own
takes on a life it learned
before our backs were turned:
when we are here alone,
the wood reverts to trees,
forests we garden in.
At first, the space between

the trees echoes with caution:
we coax them into motion,
familiar flowers rise,
old promises revise
themselves in whispered caution.
But then some gesture of the wind,
            a falling log
in the fire, a drift of fog

across the windowpane,
breathes toward some old refrain
we once had thought to speak.
Plainly the forest wakes;
now in the windowpane
flash quick reflections of light birds;
            a small wind sifts
among the trees and lifts

the undersides of leaves.
Imagined air unweaves
our losses and dissolves
ourselves into ourselves,
scatters us into leaves,
and you and I become
whatever words we may
have come so far to say.

Green Springs the Tree

My young son lurches halfway down the stair
or shrieks and totters midway through a climb
from the wobbling bookcase to the rocking chair.
I freeze and hold my breath. Most of the time
I am too far away to break the fall
that seldom comes. Instead, I stoop and bend
with him, as if threads of remote control
could reel out and connect him to my hand
that strains against his fall, against my leap
to rescue him. My twisting body prays
for skill in this, the high wire he will keep
both of us on as we rehearse the ways
to braid these strands of our inheritance
and teach poor body english how to dance.

The Flying Change

1

The canter has two stride patterns, one on the right lead and one on the left, each a mirror image of the other. The leading foreleg is the last to touch the ground before the moment of suspension in the air. On cantered curves, the horse tends to lead with the inside leg. Turning at liberty, he can change leads without effort during the moment of suspension, but a rider's weight makes this more difficult. The aim of teaching a horse to move beneath you is to remind him how he moved when he was free.

2

A single leaf turns sideways in the wind
in time to save a remnant of the day;
I am lifted like a whipcrack to the moves
I studied on that barbered stretch of ground,
before I schooled myself to drift away

from skills I still possess, but must outlive.
Sometimes when I cup water in my hands
and watch it slip away and disappear,
I see that age will make my hands a sieve;
but for a moment the shifting world suspends

its flight and leans toward the sun once more,
as if to interrupt its mindless plunge
through works and days that will not come again.
I hold myself immobile in bright air,
sustained in time astride the flying change.

Projectile Point, Circa 2500 BCE

In the garden in high summer as the sun dropped,
I worked my hoe in short scythe-swings
until one stroke turned a pebble I stopped to pick up.
I stood pinching it, thumbing off earth crumbs;

this has happened before, but not to me.
There were dozens of these in a black japanned box
in my grandfather's bedroom, which was also
his grandfather's bedroom. In the days when men

plowed the fields behind horses, sunup to sundown
watching the furrow open up and lie over,
three paces ahead of their feet, there was time
to reach down midstride and pocket a recognized stone.

At such times a man might fall to imagining,
but why not stick to such facts as may be?
It is broken at tip and base: botched,
chipped at the end of a shaft-flight,

or lost until it broke under the plow;
and such facts as there are now include
one hot afternoon when I stood sole-deep
in soft ground, wondering at the four thousand years

between the two men who had touched this stone,
guessing how it was not to care
for the magic I felt flowing out of it,
but just to stand here, touching only an implement

like a hoe or a pitchfork, watching the ground
as I watched it, not thinking of the sun
moving on as it moved over me, as it will
when the rocks and the water are alone here again.

Hawk

Last year I learned to speak to a red-tail hawk.
He wheeled above me as I crossed a field;
he screamed; I pulled a blade of grass, set it
against my lips, and started screaming back.

We held that conversation for half a mile.
Once in a while he calls me out of the house
and I comb a border for the right blade of grass.
I used to wish I might learn what it is

we mean to one another; now, I keep
the noise we've mastered for itself alone,
for glimpses of his descent toward dead elms,
and a heart that will not mind when I am gone.

Not Yet

The day may come when I will sit in a chair and stare
    myself slowly away,
or stand still at the edge of a field or the end
    of an unfamiliar street
grappling for the memory that might seem to make long
    life worthwhile,

but today, almost dozing in noon sun, I blinked and
    looked down the driveway
in time to see six deer come over the fence out of
    nowhere, their sharp feet
barely printing the ground, and melt into woods
    toward absolute purity of style.

At the Swings

Midafternoon in Norfolk,
late July. I am taking our two sons for a walk
away from their grandparents' house; we have
directions to a miniature playground,
and I have plans to wear them down
toward a nap at five,

when my wife and I
will leave them a while with her father. A few blocks
south of here, my wife's mother drifts from us
beneath hospital sheets, her small strength bent
to the poisons and the rays they use
against a spreading cancer.

In their house now, deep love
is studying to live with deepening impatience
as each day gives our hopes a different form
and household tasks rise like a powdery mist
of restless fatigue. Still, at five,
my wife and I will dress

and take the boulevard
across the river to a church where two dear friends
will marry; rings will be blessed, promises kept
and made, and while our sons lie down to sleep,
the groom's niece, as the flower girl,
will almost steal the show.

But here the boys have made
an endless procession on the slides, shrieking down
slick steel almost too hot to touch; and now
they charge the swings. I push them from the front,
one with each hand, until at last
the rhythm, and the sunlight

that splashes through live oak
and crape myrtle, dappling dead leaves on the ground,
lull me away from this world toward a state
still and remote as an old photograph
in which I am standing somewhere
I may have been before:

there was this air, this light,
a day of thorough and forgetful happiness;
where was it, or how long ago? I try
to place it, but it has gone for good,
to leave me gazing at these swings,
thinking of something else

I may have recognized—
an irrecoverable certainty that now,
and now, this perfect afternoon, while friends
are struggling to put on their cutaways
or bridal gowns, and my wife's mother,
dearer still, is dozing

after her medicine,
or turning a small thing in her mind, like someone
worrying a ring of keys to make small sounds
against great silence, and while these two boys
swing back and forth against my hand,
time's crosshairs quarter me

no matter where I turn.
Now it is time to go. The boys are tired enough,
and my wife and I must dress and go to church.
Because I love our friends, and ceremony,
the usual words will make me weep:
hearing the human prayers

for holy permanence
will remind me that a life is much to ask
of anyone, yet not too much to give

to love. And once or twice, as I stand there,
    that dappled moment at the swings
        will rise between the lines,

        when I beheld our sons
as, in the way of things, they will not be again,
    though even years from now their hair may lift
    a little in a breeze, as if they stood
        somewhere along their way from us,
            poised for a steep return.

V

Breakings and An Afternoon of Pocket Billiards

(1962–1975)

And so no force, however great, can stretch a cord, however fine, into a horizontal line which shall be absolutely straight.

—William Whewell, *Elementary Treatise on Mechanics* (1819)

Breakings

Long before I first left home, my father
tried to teach me horses, land, and sky,
to show me how his kind of work was done.
I studied how to be my father's son,
but all I learned was, when the wicked die,
they ride combines through barley forever.

Every summer I hated my father
as I drove hot horses through dusty grass;
and so I broke with him, and left the farm
for other work, where unfamiliar weather
broke on my head an unexpected storm
and things I had not studied came to pass.

So nothing changes, nothing stays the same,
and I have returned from a broken home
alone, to ask for a job breaking horses.
I watch a colt on a longe line making
tracks in dust, and think of the kinds of breakings
there are, and the kinds of restraining forces.

December Love Song

Outside the diner, snow
   muffles the lighted street.
You sit before me now,
and I, through smoke and steam,
   stare at your lips, repeat
not yours, but words I dream
   you send above the chink
   of forks and plates. I shrink,

become a boy of eight
   perched on a washing machine:
close to our inadequate
and antiquated radio,
   I dream my ears as keen
as those of stern-lipped Tonto
   warning the Lone Ranger
   of imperceptible danger.

All my childish wishes
   concentrate on static,
the clatter of the dishes
in the sink before my mother,
   the roar of the automatic
washing machine, all other
   disruptive sounds that can
   drown out the tall Masked Man

and the Indian, the sounds
   from good and bad guys' guns.
My heart is out of bounds
now, beyond the swinging door,
   beyond the cinnamon buns
untouched on the plate before
   your eyes that try to reach
   beyond attempts at speech,

back with the drum of hooves,
   the note of recognition—
as the White Horse Silver moves
across the plain, following
   the wind and the donation
of the Bullet—in the bellowing
   of one proud man who knows
   the Masked Man and tells those

who wondered who this was
   whose ringing voice is dying
now. Outside, the snow is
falling on the street, on eyes,
   the White Horse Silver, lying
on lips, your voice that tries
   to reach across this table, where
   it dies, drowned out in static air.

Among the Departures from This House

In Coke bottles waiting to be returned,
under the faded couch, beside the bed,
in empty cups that perch about the room,

dust settles, gathers, breeds, and comes alive.
It grows like snow—nothing improves before
the slow and tactless onslaught of my hands,

until, as I lie sifting toward sleep,
the little balls of dust unite, fall in,
move out like lemmings, marching against the wind.

An Afternoon of Pocket Billiards

Here where there is neither hope nor haste
all my days blend; each dark day is misplaced
        inside my crowded head.
I try to beat a game, half chance, half cold
and steady practice, struggling for the skill
that might kill chance. But chance's claws take hold,
the game is wrecked, and time is all I kill:
no sleight of hand or heart can overcome
the fear that, in this darkness, only time
        is not already dead.

I narrow down my gaze to where I waste
days growing used to a dusty taste
        that hangs in the dead air;
motes of chalk and talcum powder sift
down past the hard edge of the swinging light
above my table. Jukebox voices drift
by me through the dark, raveled with a slight
vibration from that older world beyond
the window: now I listen for a sound
        that may still rise somewhere

        this afternoon, away
from here . . . my eyes wander from where I play
to the motions of more skillful hands than mine:
another player leans above his cue.
Between us, those old tremors seem to move
the air I stare through, almost as if you
were breathing here: that half-remembered love
        obscures the perfect shot
I turned to watch; I turn back, but am caught
between my past and the shifting design

on a green field of order where I wait
for time and strength of will to dissipate
        these shapes that coil and turn
above the hush and click of herded spheres.
Brief glimpses of a chain of treacheries
flicker around a melody that bears
into this room the gradual disease
we fled when you tore blindly out our driveway
for the last time, and I came here to play,
        to wait for your return,

for this game's random shifts to bring you back
or set me free. As I blunder through each rack,
        no two shots are the same;
yet if, beneath them all, dim certainties
evolve to hold my called shots on a course
that weaves beyond love's sudden vagaries,
still, an impulse like love, in the force
behind that wavering song, caroms my thought
into an old mistake: with every shot
        I call, I speak your name.

High and low, striped and solid balls rotate
in endless formations as time grows late.
        My concentration breaks
just at the dead-reckoned instant before
each shot: testing stroke and angle, I ease
down on the felt and line it up once more;
too late, I feel that slight vibration seize
my arm—too late to stand. My knocking heart
shatters skill and chance, and takes the game apart.
    I make my own mistakes.

I chalk my cue and call for one more rack,
believing I might still untwist the wreck
        your song makes in my head.
I think how spellbound Bottom woke to shout

through nightmare trees, "When my cue comes, call me,
and I will answer. . . ." Your voice might find me out,
note by note unraveling to recall me
from this enchanted wood beyond your reach.
"When my cue comes. . . ." Moving only by touch,
          I try to hold the thread,

listening for the words to an old song
that draws me down, sets me adrift among
          patterns below the game.
The words will not connect. Red blood and bone,
older than love, the swirling echo drives
me down below green felt toward solid stone
whose grains read out the sequence of my lives
in sounds like underwater footsteps. My blind
and whispering fingers stroke the stone to find
          strength to forget the shame

I learned too long ago. I may be wrong
to follow an ancient, dimly sounding song
          whose melody is fear,
whose words might never speak; but now I know
that in it, somewhere, forces of hand and will
combine like dancers on a stage. And now,
within the strictness of my touch, I feel
a surge of steadiness. I rise to air,
to dust and vacant noise and old despair.
          Error still holds me here,

          but I'll be right someday:
though one song of old love has died away,
an older song is falling into place.
From now on I will play to make it speak,
to see the form its words give to this game.
I see, as I move into another rack,
that all days in this cavern are the same:
          endless struggles to know

how cold skill and a force like love can flow
together in my veins, and be at peace.

Here where there is neither hope nor haste
I narrow down my gaze to where I waste
          this afternoon away;
on a green field of order, where I wait
for this game's random shifts to bring you back,
high and low, striped and solid balls rotate.
I chalk my cue and call for one more rack,
listening for the words to an old song
I learned too long ago: "I may be wrong,
          but I'll be right someday."

The Hughesville Scythe

The hills where I grew up had learned to hide
destructions from each other long before
Hughesville saw destruction take its store,
and still the Hughesville legend has not died:

how once the storekeeper unlocked the door
to find he had been robbed. One clue, beside
the hearth, a swallow's nest on the stone floor,
told him how the burglar had got inside.

The old man took a scythe-blade from his store
and fixed it in the chimney, across the fine-
edged dark, where it would split a man who tried
to come that way again and steal his gold.

No burglar ever came. Now those designs
are choked in honeysuckle, and the old
insistent rituals of decay unfold:
yet in my brain that unused blade still shines,

and when I try to walk through dark I hold
my hand before me, touching solid signs,
thinking how a man can hunt for gold
and lie in pieces in the raging vines.

Pastoral

for David R. Slavitt

In the country, you learn to live at peace
with your neighbor; he is farther away,
but when you meet, you always stop and talk.

You learn that he is a pathologist
who every day kisses his wife goodbye
and goes to the lab, and blows up a goat.

The trees grow up around you as he speaks.

Afterwards, he counts the fragments, notes
their average size, and calculates the impact
with which they struck the walls.
                                                            In the evening,
you might hear him mowing his lawn, or closing
his garage door for the night. Cricket sounds
surround you both out here; in the morning,
when you pass him on the road, you smile and wave.

Snapshot

So huge he couldn't reach below his belt
(he'd been a sideshow fat man for a while),
Mr. Shipman always kept a boy with him
whose job, whenever he was called upon,
was to unbutton that enormous fly,
reach in and grab, then stand aside and aim.
Once, behind the grandstand at a ball game,
while Shipman shifted his impatient flesh
from foot to foot, the boy groped in the trousers
and said, "Mr. Shipman, I can't find it." "Well,
God damn it, boy, you the last man had it."

Riding Lesson

I learned two things
from an early riding teacher.
He held a nervous filly
in one hand and gestured
with the other, saying "Listen.
Keep one leg on one side,
the other leg on the other side,
and your mind in the middle."

He turned and mounted.
She took two steps, then left
the ground, I thought for good.
But she came down hard, humped
her back, swallowed her neck,
and threw her rider as you'd
throw a rock. He rose, brushed
his pants and caught his breath,
and said, "See, that's the way
to do it. When you see
they're gonna throw you, get off."

Toad

Squat in the stagnant sunlight
on the moss beneath a shrub
its tongue slowly flicking
its throat slowly throbbing
huddled alone in the wood.
A ten-year-old boy exploring
found it damp and sparkling there
and caught it up in his hands.
He felt the frightened
water on his fingers.
Into his pocket carefully
so he could carry it home
and down on the floor he played
making it hop for his joy.
But the room was too dry
it heaved for air and died
dust clinging to its skin.
Weeping he knelt on the floor
holding this love in his fingers
waiting for someone to speak.
Before he went to bed
he put it in a box
and hid it in his closet
behind a baseball glove.

Buildings and Grounds

for Richard Dillard

The house we moved into has been landscaped
so that it has the portable, plastic look
of a Sears, Roebuck toy farm.

All up and down our street, the same minor artist seems
to have been at work; our neighbors' lawns are
watered and mowed truly until they are carpets,

their shrubs are lovingly trimmed and shaped
into green velvet eggs and spheres.
Our neighbors watch us like hawks,

wondering whether we have the equipment,
the know-how, the spirit, to strive with them
as they strive with their landscapes.

Oh, let me bring my home from the South to this street!
I will let the grass grow until it is knee-high,

I will import chickens and a blue-tick hound to trample
the grass and dig bone-holes and scratch-holes,

I will set up on cinderblocks in the front yard
a '38 Ford with no tires or headlights,

I will sit in the gutted driver's seat
with a bottle of Old Mr. Mac, glaring at my
neighbors, reading aloud from *God's Little Acre,*

I will be a prophet of wildness and sloth!

But the Puritan gaze of my neighbors cuts through
my desperate vision of home—my dream house
will not flourish here.

I will spend my rapidly declining years
    reading the labels on bags of crabgrass killer,

pushing my lawnmower until my front yard
    is as smooth as a green on a golf course,

clipping and shaping my landlord's opulent shrubs.

But don't misunderstand me—I have not been
    converted; I will still make something
    to sustain me here in this alien land.

I will plant mint in the flowerbeds beside
    the Shasta daisies we brought from Monticello,

I will set up a croquet course on the front lawn
    with a slender drink-stand at each wicket
    to hold my frosty mint juleps,

I will station an iron jockey by the driveway
    to stare back into the pitiless eyes
    of my neighbors' pink plastic flamingoes,

I will keep a Tennessee Walking Horse in the garage
    and give him a foxhound for company,

I will stand out front in a white linen suit,
    surveying my plantation,

I will plant a magnolia tree.

But now, at the height of my visionary ecstasy,
    the telephone rings. It is the man
    next door, calling to let me know

that my sprinkler is turned up too high
    and is sprinkling the seats of his convertible.

I go out to turn down the water, and I see
    that the cedar needs trimming again,
    that the elm twigs need to be raked.

I will do those things. I will hoe and trench
    and weed, I will mow the grass.
    I have moved in here now,

and I have to do what I can.

To Hear My Head Roar

First, my father taught me to read poetry
aloud; then my teachers in grade school
remembered how he had recited poetry,

how many times he had brought down the school-
house with "Casey at the Bat." Whenever they
could they called me up before the whole school

to be my father's son. I still dream of days they
stood me shaking before my classmates, then
waited while I launched into what they

knew from long experience was coming, then
sat through "Jabberwocky" or "Excelsior"—that was
the full range of my repertory then.

Later I almost liked it, though I was
still forced to it: each week we all recited
at assembly. A terrible, tiring time that was

for my audience, and for me, as I recited
"The Highwayman" and "The Cremation of
Sam McGee." My father coached as I recited

nightly in the living room, and on the day of
my graduation from that place, my sister
and I recited, respectively, "The Ballad of

the Harp-Weaver" and "The Highwayman." My sister
and I fled to our father's side after
it was over, and I can still see my sister

blushing as the old ladies came up after
the performance with tears in their eyes
to tell my father he was wonderful. After

that, it was a long time before my eyes
would follow the tricks of poems, but now I know
dozens of them: they unscroll behind my eyes,

and I own hundreds of books in which I know
I can always find the right thing at the right time,
and I will read to anyone who doesn't know

what he is in for, for hours at a time.
When I try to understand this part of myself,
I think back to that earlier, troublesome time

to find that the explanation of myself
does not lie there entirely; for now I recall being
in high school, just beginning to take myself

seriously, and my father as a human being,
and I think of hours I spent in the attic
rummaging through old file cases, being

surprised to find, in the dark dust of that attic,
the poems my father had written when he
was in college. One afternoon in the attic

yielded an ancient treasure, a recording he
had once made and then forgotten. I
tiptoed out of the attic with it, thinking he

might take it from me, and secretly I
tried it, at first without success, on the machine
downstairs in the living room. At last I

even tried to start the reluctant machine
on the inner end of the groove. It worked.
The thing had been cut on some amateur's machine

and was made to run from the inside out. I worked
with the needle, nudging it over the cracks,
and heard, after what seemed hours of work,

a voice that I recognized, through dusty cracks
and thirty years, as my father's (or my own), say
something I now take to heart as my heart cracks:

"This is Tom Taylor talking; talking," I heard him say,
"to hear his own voice, and reading some poetry
because he wants to have something to say."

Riding a One-Eyed Horse

One side of his world is always missing.
You may give it a casual wave of the hand
or rub it with your shoulder as you pass,
but nothing on his blind side ever happens.

Hundreds of trees slip past him into darkness,
drifting into a hollow hemisphere
whose sounds you will have to try to explain.
Your legs will tell him not to be afraid

if you learn never to lie. Do not forget
to turn his head and let what comes come seen:
he will jump the fences he has to if you swing
toward them from the side that he can see

and hold his good eye straight. The heavy dark
will stay beside you always; let him learn
to lean against it. It will steady him
and see you safely through diminished fields.

Smoking in Bed in the Fire Chief's House

A gull drops clams on rocks
near where I lie taking what sun
there is above Nantucket, lulled almost
to sleep by the sound of waves, kept
awake by the thud of clams

on sand, and the rattling
sigh of salt-grass on the moors.
As the gull rises and falls, flickering in
and out of the corner of my eye,
the beach becomes the sheet

of my rented bed in town,
held as if by a ring of men. In a dull
daze between sleep and waking, I think the sheet
is slackened and pulled taut by hunters
in the north—they toss the gull,

the lightest hunter, high
into the air, so that from his perch
on nothing he can search for the blowhole
of the seal, the shifting whiteness
of the polar bear.

Closer to sleep, I become
the sharp-eyed hunter, tossed from the blanket
in time with waves; I rise above, then fall
below the gull, who hangs motionless
in the air beyond the rail

of the rolling ferry
that brought me here; he drifts
in and out of my field of vision as the boat
rocks slowly over the waves, lifting
me out of troughs, above

the waves, to look toward
the land I fled, as it recedes
into the distance beyond the stationary gull,
before I am caught, let down, then tossed
again to train my eyes

on the land beyond the shore,
to search out the quarry, whatever
it was I fled when I embarked. Driving
down the gangplank from the parking hold,
I carry glimpses of the world

I left behind—a face,
a cold flame around my heart, burning
images reduced to ash by time and distance:
glimpses that will fade, then blaze up,
as I drive to my rented room

in Irving Bartlett's house.
His wife shows me where things are; she points
at last to a brass gong above my bedroom door.
"It rings," she says, "whenever there's
a fire. My husband is

the Fire Chief here." So far,
it has clattered every day, only
to let the whole town know the noon hour
has arrived—there has been no alarm
set off by burning house

or tree, or by the flame
I cannot kindle in my brain.
Here nothing burns—not even my pale skin
in slant sunlight. I pray for sparks,
but nothing catches fire

inside me or around me
as I ride the sounds of gulls and waves
to sleep, to dream myself astride a borrowed horse,
riding across the moors, listening
for gabbling beagles smoking

over a scent laid down
by hares. Beneath the horse's hooves
soft sand gives way along the beach where I lie
asleep, dreaming now of lying awake
with a lighted cigarette

in the Fire Chief's house,
thinking how the room might blaze around me
if I should fall asleep—how a fire might catch
hold of me once more, to wrap me
in tongues until my voice

could sing a name for the face
that chars within me. A *clack* beside
my head snaps me awake; I throw the broken
clam away, out over a rail that blurs
as sleep recedes toward

the shore I cannot see.
Awake at last, I watch this land
shine from the waves for the first time since I came.
The face I fled is ashes now,
and I can love the gull

who drops toward the clam
I threw out over moors where beagles
blaze over the trail of the hare, their voices
ringing in my ears, mingling with
the fire bell and the waves

        until their flaming tongues
    fill the air above the moors with song.
The face I wanted to name becomes this landscape,
    named forever only by the sea.
        My tongue on fire at last,

        I rise from this beach,
    turning toward the flame-touched song
of hounds. Under their smoking breath, in the wind,
    the salt-grass burns on the sand
        dunes, blade by blade.

Harvest

Every year in late July I come back to where I was raised,
to mosey and browse through old farm buildings,
over fields that seem never to change,

rummaging through a life I can no longer lead
and still cannot leave behind, looking for relics
that might spring back to that life at my touch.

Today, among thistles and ragweed, I stumble on
a discarded combine—the old kind we pulled
with a tractor to cut and thresh barley and wheat.

Now it lies listing into the side of this hill
like a stone or an uprooted stump, harboring snakes
and wasps, rusting slowly down into the briars.

Still, I climb to the seat, wondering whether it will
hold me, fumbling for pedals and levers
I used to know by heart. Above my head,

the grain-pipe forks down to the bag-clamps,
and a wad of tie-strings, gone weedy and rotten,
still hangs by my right hand. As I touch these things,

this machine I once knew by many unprintable names
moves out through barley in late July, and the stalks
fall to the knife as the paddle-reel sweeps them in.

On wide canvas belts, cut grain rides into the dark
insides of the combine, where frantic shakers and screens
break the grain loose from the stalks and the chaff;

almost invisible, small spines from the grain-heads
pour out through holes in the metal, billowing
into a cloud that moves with us over the hills,

engulfing me, the machine, the tractor and driver,
 as we work in a spiral to the center of the field,
 rolling back through the years in a dust cloud.

The spines stick to my skin, work into my pores,
 my bloodstream, and finally blaze into my head
 like a miniature cactus of hatred for all grain,

for flour and cereal and bread, for mildewed surplus
 swelling in midwestern silos. Never again,
 I thought once, as I rode out the cloud until sundown,

never again. I climb down and walk out through the thistles,
 still breathing fifteen-year-old barley. The years
 in the cloud drift back to me. Metal rusts into the hill.

Barley-dust pricks at my brain, and I am home.

Burning a Horse

We watch him burn—
hoof, hide, and bone.
—James Seay

Riding on a flatbed wagon, carrying with us
an ax, pitchforks, a coil of heavy rope,
and a five-gallon can of kerosene,

we went to the back meadow that afternoon,
driven to desperate measures
by the stench that hung on the still air,

dead air that lay like fog in the valley
around us, not enough motion in it even
to carry buzzards whose random glide

might have brought them to the body
of the Percheron that festered on the grass
where we had dragged him after he had died.

We spent an hour cutting brush from fallen trees,
carrying it to where the horse lay bulging
in the sun; we hooked him to the tractor

and pulled him over the pile of brush,
to get it under him, then soaked
the brushpile and his body with the kerosene.

I threw a match into the trembling vapors
that rose from the fuel and from the rotting
horse, then dropped back as the explosion

blasted us with the smell of burning hair. Slowly,
one patch of skin, then another, burned through
to let the gas escape and blaze like a blowtorch,

but the flames died down too soon, and we could hear
the flesh speaking, one of the men said, as
a cornfield does, growing after a hard rain.

We ran up to the pyre with more brush, holding
our breath as we used pitchforks to place
the dry sticks where they seemed needed most,

and then saw fire catch the wood, the flesh,
and saw black smoke so thick and heavy
that it hid us from each other; it crawled

down the meadow a few feet above the ground,
the smell we held our breath against
tainting everything it touched. Burning at last,

the horse was blackening and shrinking into the tall
meadow grass; and then, before us, there,
from coals that had caught hold in the horse's bones,

we saw a horse, made whole, with heavy flesh
and shining skin, rippling against the pull,
rising from the grass around the dying fire,

his new hoofs shod, his mane flying, rising
from the coals and moving in a smooth
and dangerous way; he traveled down the meadow

at a sweeping gallop, wrapped in something
like a flame, light and heat around him
that did not flicker or drop from him as he disappeared.

The sun rolled down the hill above the meadow,
and in the dusk a wind came up.
We strained our eyes, but the horse was gone,

moving perhaps beyond the stand of willow trees
at the upper end of the meadow, carrying
the light around him into darkness beyond our view.

We turned to look at the spot where the fire
        had been, listening for the crackling
        of smoldering bones, but all we heard

was our own blood and breath, and the sound
        of the wind that must have carried him away. Ashes
        lifted slowly in that wind, like heavy wings.

Miss Creighton

was still, somewhere in her seventies, among
the last and toughest of the singlehanded
farmers in the country around our house.

In the wind, her long blue dress would ripple
and snap about her high-top shoes, as she rode
her hayrake hard behind her two black Percherons.

One day, years ago, we stood at the gate
and watched her working the field
half a mile away;

and when she saw us, she lifted the rake-teeth,
waved and yelled, whirled
the long black reins above her head,

and sent those heavy horses over the hills
toward us at a lumbering run—her blue sleeves

luffed like sails, the rake's steel wheels
touched the ground only once in a while.

At the gate, she gazed toward where she'd been,
and as she rolled her words
across the air between us,

Scotland's dark blue hills took shape upon those fields
where she worked alone to raise her beef,
to clear her hilly land of rocks.

"It does good where I pick them up," she said,
"and where I put them down."

Today, the last black Angus has been sold,
the last stray stone has found its place.

Her Percherons, unharnessed now, walk side by side
        across the fields, toward what rose
        whenever she spoke:

they lean together for the last time into the pull,
        moving away from us
        over the dark blue hills of Scotland.

An Old Rhodes Scholar

Arthur Kyle Davis, Jr. (1897–1972)

Holding seminars at bay
with stern requirements and sly questioning
grows dull as days grow longer; spring
brings back an earlier time. Thoughts go astray.

He finds himself gazing
beyond the aging trees outside his window
at a man his friends no longer know,
a strong-armed youth poised at the end of a blazing

playing field, stretching, warming
up, pacing off the runway, his tape-wound
bamboo pole beside him on the ground.
So long ago. He blinks to shake off swarming

visions that always return
to catch him napping: he lifts the vaulting pole
toward the bar, begins to roll
forward on his left foot to start his run.

Slowly the upper end
of the pole descends toward the mark
and he is raised in a sunlit arc
to the trembling bar. He hoists his feet, bends

his waist, then hangs, jack-
knife, above the sawdust pit for an instant
too perfect for the crowd of distant
admirers to believe, straightens his back,

then, like a cruising bird
that hunts for miles with hungry eyes to find
a furred or feathered something on the ground
and finally dives on widespread unheard

wings to earth, descends
to stand once more before these youthful faces.
He fumbles with his notes, retraces
his steps, once more begins what never ends

until those early days
return, unbidden, to interrupt a lecture
on Wordsworth or the architecture
of an ode by Keats. Once more he turns away

toward the window, pride
trembling in his voice as he recalls
some old contest. The classroom falls
away to let us see him pausing, dignified,

immaculate in tweeds,
his old-fashioned bamboo pole in his hands,
ready to begin his run. He stands
a moment, thinking, then his right foot leads

him toward the bar again,
while we, who have known him only in that room,
are now amazed to see him in the bloom
of age, his paisley tie and gold stickpin

flawlessly in place
as he picks up speed along the cinder runway,
rises once more toward the bar, away
from rooms and lives he filled with ease and grace.

Bernard and Sarah

"Hang them where they'll do some good," my grandfather
said, as he placed the dusty photograph
in my father's hands. My father and I stared
at two old people posed stiffly side by side—
my great-great-great-grandparents, in the days
when photography was young, and they were not.
My father thought it out as we drove home.

Deciding that they might do the most good
somewhere out of sight, my father drove
a nail into the back wall of his closet;
they have hung there ever since, brought out
only on such occasions as the marriage
of one of his own children. "I think you ought
to know the stock you're joining with," he says.

Then back they go to the closet, where they hang
keeping their counsel until it is called for.
Yet, through walls, over miles of fields and woods
that flourish still around the farm they cleared,
their eyes light up the closet of my brain
to draw me toward the place I started from,
and when I have come home, they take me in.

VI

The Horse Show at Midnight (1963–1966)

. . . and yet if you ride confidently and well, and ask confidently and soundly for your horse's best level of performance, his response will be to the ride you give him, and not to your secret thoughts.

—William Steinkraus, *Riding and Jumping*

Blackberries

On top of a ragged hill on the farm
Next to my father's, an old man
Sat on his front porch and reigned
Over a dominion of thistles and briars.

In his meadow, never mowed,
Blackberries grew wild, overran
The field, smothered the grass,
Bound the cows and ate them alive.

My sisters and I would steal
Under his fence, armed with pails,
To pick as many berries as we could.
We never got them all, hard as we tried.

One afternoon we stood in the briars
Reaching for berries over our heads,
Each one hanging before us like a bunch
Of grapes, when down from his porch

The old man tumbled, down the hill
Toward us, wild white hair in the wind,
Scattering all of his chickens as he ran.
His tiny dog yapped at his heels.

"Go back where you belong right now!"
And he waved his arms. We turned
And ran for the fence, clutching the pails
In our arms, scattering berries behind us.

We looked back once and saw him on the hill,
Shaking his fist in the wind and shouting.
"If you're too lazy to raise your own blackberries,
By God, you shan't have mine!"

A Blind Man Locking His House

The tall clock in the hallway strikes
The half-hour chime:
Twelve-thirty. Now the hour has come
For footsteps in the dark, that like
To wander through this house from room to room.

My wife and I live here alone,
So my wife thinks;
But in the dark my dark eye blinks,
Down passageways of pure unknown
The hunter starts to stalk, and my heart sinks.

I rise and gird myself to face
This sounding house,
One hand stretched out against the blows
From chairs that will not stay in place,
From anarchy that sightlessness allows,

The other rummaging for keys
In my coat pocket.
At each door, as I pause to lock it,
Relentless blood assails my eyes
And drives them crazy: useless in their sockets,

They still roll upward in my head.
By force of will
I aim them downward: through this chill,
Pretending to look straight ahead,
I make the footsteps think I see, until

Between me and this heavy tread
At least one door
Is safely locked. From door to door
I pass, and learn I am misled:
There is no safe place for me any more.

To such thoughts does this presence tempt me
As floorboards creak
That I might drive myself to break
My heart at last, and find it empty,
Because some thing stalks me and will not speak.

The hallway clock clangs like my heart,
In time with feet
That flee, and press behind, and meet
At last, and all of this is part
Of all this house. My pitiful conceit

Breaks down, and I shall not escape.
Older than air
Or the stairway, he is somewhere
In dust and stone that saps all hope;
When I lie down that sound will still be there.

Time and again my wife has said
No one is there;
But in the weather of despair
As I climb up through dark to bed
I hear his step behind me on the stair.

Things Not Solved Though Tomorrow Came

> For whether lighted over ways that save,
> Or lured from all repose,
> If he go on too far to find a grave,
> Mostly alone he goes.
> —E. A. Robinson

There is silence in this blue car now.
My daughter and I have driven for hours
Through early morning, where we started,
High noon on the turnpike, where we stopped
To eat in a pink brick restaurant,
On through to afternoon, the hour when
The sun shines on the sides of golden things,
Until we are struck dumb by nearness to the end,
The long green shadows of her boarding school
Where we are bound, where we arrive at last.

We unload the car in several trips,
Carrying up the stairs to the third floor
Her clothes, her blankets, pennants, lamps,
Stuffed animals. The job at last is done.
She stands before me, smiling, as I lean
Against the car, my hand on my thick waist,
Trying not to sweat or gasp for breath.
It is time for me to leave. She kisses me
On the forehead.
"Goodbye, sweetheart," I say.
"We'll miss you. Hit the books. Write home some time."

She kisses me once more, then walks away.
I think of last year at this time,
Her first year here, when neither she
Nor I could keep tears back for long.
She walks across the dying, dark green grass,
Her brown hair, her mother's hair, shining

As it comes between my eyes and the sun.
Some friends of hers are waiting on the porch—
A tall boy smiles, and she begins
To line up love in the nick of time.

Autumn is descending on this hemisphere;
Leaves are turning now, in Pennsylvania.
The sun is shining on the sides of things,
And another summer has come to an end.
I climb into my car and turn for home—
I have far to go, and not much time.
My daughter's face is formed inside my mind
And I say to it,
"When you were born,
Light of my life, I could not in
My wildest dreams imagine you like this."

I am alone in my blue car once more.
You are home safe, and I turn south
Trying to retain some sense of your presence
At my side, some sound, but all I hear
Is silence deeper than our speechlessness.
My mind turns slowly back through these
Brown leaves, to autumns of my childhood.

In the cellar, in a spacious crate,
I kept a lamb until it died.
My father gave me another, and I tried
To feed it clover blooms and bottled milk.
I fed it every morning, every night.
One winter Saturday I slept late;
When I awoke, the sun was high, shone
Through dead leaves of trees outside my window.
I rose and heated the bottle of milk,
Went down the stairs and stood on my toes
To lean over the side of the crate.

The lamb lay still, would not arise.
I stood there for what may have been an hour,
Staring down at those dull and dusty eyes,
And thought of rabbits I had kept out back
The year before, and how the babies bled
To death one night when a weasel
Got through a hole I had not patched that day.

Darkness comes upon me on the road.
Before I assail the windy turnpike
I have to stop for coffee, noise, and light.
There is a diner up ahead, next to a motel
That advertises Rest for Weary Bones.
Inside, the clock above the smoking grill
Says eight-fifteen. I take a booth beside
The window, and watch the highway wind away.
A young girl brings a menu and a glass
Of water and stands above me, pencil poised,
Moving in time to the jukebox music
Which I had not heard until I looked at her.

I order only coffee. As she turns
Away she winks and asks me if I'm tired.
Daughter, your feet upon the dying grass
Did not move as hers do, dancing on these tiles.

When she returns she slides into the booth
Across from me, searches for three jukebox tunes
To spend my quarter on, and, as she touches
My hand and smiles, I see through coffee steam
And smoke the eyes that looked through me at lunch
This afternoon;
                                they tell me I have far
To go, but I have stopped for now.
                                                        She lifts
The little jar of cream that I had left
Untouched beside the sugar bowl, holds it

Before her face as if to offer me
A toast, then drinks it down in one small gulp.

She smiles, and we sit talking now about
Where I have been, where I am going, how
She likes her work, and why she does it.
The things I say are of no consequence,
Regardless of the effort I have made.
I forget words as I speak them, only note
Her nod, her eyes, how hard it is for me
To keep my daughter's voice from drowning hers,
To keep the world beyond the foggy window
From moving through the dark outside until
The lines that hold me to it are cast off
At last, and I am left with nothing but
Her face, the things our fingers touch, words I forget. . . .

Daughter, I speak to her of you, say you
Are beautiful, think to myself that you
Must never know how, when I speak,
Hers becomes the face whose eyes I praise.

Hours, cigarettes, and cups of coffee
Find us sitting at this table still,
Her fingers touching mine.
                                        The man behind
The counter tells us it is time to leave.
I notice, as he speaks to her, a tone
Not at all familiar, as if we both
Were customers. I rise and start to say
It's Been Nice Talking To You, but no words
Come. She finds her coat and brings it to me;
I help her into it as if I had
Done so a thousand times before,
And we depart, when I have paid the man
Behind the counter, arm in arm.

We stand still outside for a moment,
Until we can see each other in this dark.
I suppose she must be twenty-five or so.
Daughter, love, I say to you I see in her
Eyes a thing I have not seen in yours,
A thing no one I've loved has let me see
For years. We do not speak.
                                        She gets into
My car while I walk across the road
To the office of the motel, speak to
Someone, pay him money, go out with the key.
Speechless in the car, we cross the road
Together, get out and stand beside the door,
My hand on her elbow.
                                    It is cold out here,
Perhaps for the first time, I tell myself,
This fall. At home, where lights have probably
Gone out, late treefrogs may be speaking still
By the pond at the end of the driveway.
You have unpacked your things and gone to bed,
Thinking perhaps of the tall boy who smiled
At you this afternoon,
                                    and I stand here
With this strange waitress, thinking thoughts I have
Not thought for years and years—
                                                how one must act
At times like this to keep the moment real,
Create a world out of thin air: to keep
Things going as they are supposed to go.

Inside, attempts at speech in the dim light
Of the desk lamp, then silence as before.
She comes into my arms for a minute
Or two, then disengages me and sits
Along the bed's edge, lights two cigarettes,

And holds one out to me ambiguously:
Daring or inviting me to sit down.
I sit down close to her and take her hand;
We smoke in silence for a time.
                                        Why did
You bring me here? I almost ask, but know
That her reply would sound the same.
                                                  She rises,
Then crosses to the desk, close to the light,
And starts to take her clothes off. I undo
My tie, then stop and look at her. Her white
Waitress's uniform, unbuttoned at
The front, slides slowly down over shoulders
And hangs about her hips.
                                    I have come far
To find this room, this creaking bed, this light
That plays such tricks upon my eyes and on
Her hands and hair;
                              I think at this moment
I shall be here forever while all things
Grow old around me, pass me in the dark,
And I shall lie tortured in this cavern
Until death, or madness, comes.
                                        But now,
Straight from a pile of clothes upon her feet
She rises, moves into my arms,
An island rising from the sea.

Now I lie here on this disheveled bed
Relaxing my tense muscles one by one.
Remembering an old consideration
Born of an old embarrassment, I try
To drift toward sleep without moving a hand
Or breathing too loudly. I fall closer
To sleep, but feel something stir in my brain

And recognize a shame from years ago,
Remembering how, at school, I stained my
Underwear behind locked doors, night after night.
Longer ago than that, I crouched at night
In bed on all fours, sitting on my feet,
And rocked back and forth singing to myself
Or dreaming of the time I would be free,
And fell, at last, forward on my face,
Put my thumb into my mouth, and fell asleep.

And at this moment, as I fall toward sleep
I sense in this tenseness in
My arm the effort to keep
My hand, my thumb, beside me.

I dream of rabbits the weasel killed,
Of lambs that died in my care.

When I wake, I am sitting up in bed.
This girl is gone, whose eyes shone with some thing
I had not seen for years till now, whose voice
Moved in me even through dark clouds of sleep.
I try to bring her face before my eyes,
But all I can remember is the way
Her dress hung on her hips as she stood before me.
It is still dark outside, and still.
In the hundred miles ahead of dark
Turnpike I will have time enough to try
To remember faces, in that roaring chill.

I lie down and light a fresh cigarette.
I roll over on my stomach and stretch,
Then drop the cigarette in one instant
Of the coldest dread, one moment so short

It could contain but one impression, to be thought
About forever after it.

In that

Instant, a giant thing stood over me:
Its legs were at my shoulders, hips and feet,
Its heavy, shining wings clapped on its back;
I do solemnly swear I heard its breath,
And felt its rasping jaws above my neck.
Oh, daughter, darling, what can this thing be?
Can it have been so wrong that you loved me?

I rise from bed and take the road once more. The car
Rolls through the darkness as a fierce beast runs through cold,
Extinguishing a whispered calling in my ear.
Of what is past, I only know what I am told:
I can no longer tell whose voice is in the air.
Headlights try for secrets the road will always hold:
There are things I have not seen though I have been to where they are.

A Dream of a Distant Land

Deep in a darkness many weeks old
I stand alone at the rail of my ship
Listening to the sounds to which
I have not yet become accustomed:
The pump of engines nudging the boat
Through the clear, cold, endless night;
The crack of icebergs that surround,
But do not bind me; and forever
The crash of water on a coast
Where seals on the rocks move slowly.
On the deck, now, I am alone,
Only thinking of you, waiting
Where thoughts of ice and whales
Are rarely more than amusements,
But I know that below me men watch
The hands of curious instruments tremble,
Hunting for the best course south
To the Arctic Circle, the open sea,
Back home to the Temperate Zones,
Where I played as a boy in the first
Cold winds of autumn among shocks
Of corn covered with frost, and walked
In the fields where my father's cattle
Lived. Through the open window
At night I could hear horses
Cantering across a field of stubble,
Steering around the shocks of corn
One night when they got out
Like polar bears cruising among
The icebergs as they swim beside
My ship in the clothing of life
Itself: claws, eyes, teeth, and hair,
Salt water running in their veins
As it runs in yours and mine.

I think of you waiting for me
In that land where summer is short
Enough to force you to remember winter.
Through the veins of the bear,
In your brain and in mine,
The blood that knows will blunder
Its way from season into season,
As it sends the fish beneath me
Through the dark, like horses
Dodging frozen white shocks of corn
On a stubble sea, their senses
Of direction trembling like the hands
On the dials of careful instruments below
That guide me to you from breaking waves
Where seals on the rocks move slowly.

ACKNOWLEDGMENTS

The selected poems herein are from *The Horse Show at Midnight* (LSU Press, 1966, 1992); *Breakings* (Solo Press, 1971); *An Afternoon of Pocket Billiards* (University of Utah Press, 1975; LSU Press, 1992), *The Flying Change* (LSU Press, 1985), *Understanding Fiction* (LSU Press, 1996), and *Crooked Run* (LSU Press, 2006).

The new poems have appeared in the following periodicals, whose hospitality to the poems and whose permission to include them here are gratefully acknowledged: *Alaska Quarterly Review,* "I Thought She Said"; *The American Scholar,* "Chapel in the Air"; *Blueline,* "Rockwell Kent on Monhegan Island"; *The Formalist,* "Yesterdays"; *Friends Journal,* "A Persuasive Chill"; *James Dickey Newsletter,* "Bird-Call at Evening"; *New Letters,* "Art and Life," "Desert Passage," "The Living Room at Springdale," and "Ultrasound"; *Poet Lore,* "Two Winter Landscapes"; *Poetry,* "For William Matthews" and "The Final Morbidity of the Interior Embezzler"; *Roanoke Review,* "A Firm Stance on Level Ground," "At the Thursday Night Jam, Remembering an Absent Singer," and "Goodbye"; *The Sewanee Review,* "Drop Us From Our Day"; *Smartish Pace,* "The Ages"; *Southern Poetry Review,* "In the Galisteo Basin"; *Tar River Poetry,* "You Don't Know All the Places You Take Me To."

The selected poems have appeared in journals as follows; grateful acknowledgment to their editors is reiterated here for their hospitality to the poems and for their permission to reprint them.

64, "Hughesville Nights"; *The American Oxonian,* "An Old Rhodes Scholar"; *Antioch Review,* "My Dear Sister Hannah"; *Atlantic Monthly,* "A Crosstown Breeze," "A Set of Hoofprints," and "After High Water"; *Beloit Poetry Journal,* "Getting Himself Together"; *Book Week,* "Breakings"; *Cargoes,* "Things Not Solved Though Tomorrow Came"; *Encounter,* "Toad"; *Folio*

(Birmingham), “Riding Lesson” and “To Hear My Head Roar”; *Folio* (American University), “A Voltage Spike” and “Within a Stone’s Throw of Greatness”; *Friends Journal,* “Snapshots”; *Georgia Review,* “An Artist from Another Place,” “Boy Hunting in Bog,” and “Metes and Bounds”; *The Hollins Critic,* “Among the Departures from This House” and “Hawk”; *Iron Horse Literary Review,* “Valentine’s Daffodils”; *LandEscapes 2000* (Washington State University), “Creek Walk”; *Michigan Quarterly Review,* “An Afternoon of Pocket Billiards”; *Mill Mountain Review,* “Miss Creighton”; *Missouri Review,* “A Little Respect” and “More Than One Way”; *New Mexico Quarterly,* “A Dream of a Distant Land”; *New Virginia Review,* “Frank Amos and the Way Things Work” and “Free Throw”; *New York Quarterly,* “Snapshot”; *Nightsun,* “On the Air”; *Ploughshares,* “Landscape with Tractor”; *Plume & Sword,* “Blackberries”; *Poetry Northwest,* “Harvest”; *Poetry,* “Master of None” and “Taking to the Woods”; *Practical Horseman* and *Carolina Quarterly,* “Riding a One-Eyed Horse”; *Sewanee Review,* “Creek Walk, ” “George Washington’s Farewell to His Hounds,” and “Understanding Fiction”; *Shenandoah,* “December Love Song” and “The Hayfork”; *Smartish Pace,* “Aka Fawn Meadow”; *Southern Poetry Review,* “Projectile Point, Circa 2500 BCE” and “The Flying Change”; *Tennessee Poetry Journal,* “Bernard and Sarah”; *The Back Door,* “Somewhere Along the Way”; *The New Republic,* “Afternoons with a Boomerang”; *The Plum Review,* “An Ending”; *The Southern Review,* “At the Grave of E. A. Robinson,” “Burning a Horse,” “Heartburn,” “Popped Balloon,” and “The Hughesville Scythe”; *Virginia Quarterly Review,* “A Straight Stretch on the Far Side of Coolbrook,” “A Trace of Old Road Work,” “At the Swings,” “Buildings and Grounds,” “Smoking in Bed in the Fire Chief’s House,” “The Dining Room at Springdale,” and “Vision at Woods’ Edge”; *Wasatch Front,* “Pastoral”; *The Washingtonian,* “Barbed Wire,” “Green Springs the Tree,” and “Learning the Language”; *Western Humanities Review,* “An Old Rhodes Scholar” and “Shapes, Vanishings.”

“As on a Darkling Plain” first appeared in *Desperado,* by Henry Taylor, in the Unicorn Folded Broadside Series. Greensboro, NC, Unicorn Press, 1979.

“After a Movie” first appeared in *Festival 88,* edited by George Garrett for the Virginia Festival of American Film, Charlottesville, 1988.

"Night Search for Lost Dog" first appeared in *Elvis in Oz: New Stories and Poems from the Hollins Creative Writing Program,* edited by Mary Flinn and George Garrett, Charlottesville, University Press of Virginia, 1992.

"Master of None" was written for the induction of new members into Phi Beta Kappa, State University of New York at Stony Brook, May, 1987; "Afternoons With a Boomerang" was the Phi Beta Kappa Poem at the College of William and Mary, December, 1992.

"My Dear Sister Hannah" is closely based on a letter from Caroline "Carrie" Taylor of Purcellville, Virginia, to her sister Hannah Stabler in Sandy Spring, Maryland. It appears in *Ye Mtg Hous Smal: A Short History of Friends in Loudoun County, Virginia, 1732–1980,* by Asa M. Janney and Werner Janney (privately printed, Lincoln, Virginia, 1980), 45–47.